Sass and Compass for Designers

Produce and maintain cross-browser CSS files easier than ever before with the Sass CSS preprocessor and its companion authoring framework, Compass

Ben Frain

PUBLISHING

BIRMINGHAM - MUMBAI

Sass and Compass for Designers

First published: April 2013

Production Reference: 1180413

Published by Packt Publishing Ltd.
Livery Place
35 Livery Street
Birmingham B3 2PB, UK.

ISBN 978-1-84969-454-4

www.packtpub.com

Cover Image by Shutter Stock

Credits

Author
Ben Frain

Project Coordinator
Joel Goveya

Reviewers
Daniel Eden

Matt Mitchell

Matt Wilcox

Proofreaders
Maria Gould

Paul Hindle

Vivienne Frain

Acquisition Editor
Edward Gordon

Indexer
Tejal Soni

Lead Technical Editor
Azharuddin Sheikh

Production Coordinator
Conidon Miranda

Technical Editors
Soumya Kanti

Dominic Pereira

Varun Pius Rodrigues

Cover Work
Conidon Miranda

Foreword

You're doing it wrong!

One day, a few years ago, I tweeted (`https://twitter.com/Malarkey/status/6435096054`):

> *"Pro tip — 'If your CSS is complicated enough to need a compiler or pre-processor, you're [sic] doing it wrong!'"*

After all, CSS isn't difficult to learn and it's easy to write and write quickly, so why would you need something like Sass?

People reacted (as they do) and told me I was wrong. They offered plenty of advice and plenty of reasons why using Sass would benefit what I do. I wasn't oblivious to their enthusiasm, so I pulled up the Sass website, ready to dive in:

> *"First of all, let's get Sass up and running. If you're using OS X, you'll already have Ruby installed. Windows users can install Ruby via the Windows installer, and Linux users can install it via their package manager."*

Oh.

> *"Once you have Ruby installed, you can install Sass by running gem install sass."*

Now you can berate me for not understanding the command line, if you like, but I'm a designer, not a developer. My degree is in Fine Art, not Computer Science. My background is print, not programming so I'll trade your ruby gems for my under-color removal and dot gain any day of the week.

How hard should this Sass thing be anyway?

```
sass --watch style.scss:style.css
sass --watch stylesheets/sass:stylesheets/compiled
```

That hard? Obviously.

My problem was that Sass documentation had typically been written by developers for developers. It used technical language and references and made assumptions about what a person wanting to get started with Sass would know. As I wasn't familiar with neither its language nor technologies I felt frustrated, stupid even, for not understanding and as a result I avoided using Sass for a long time.

Over the last few years, using HTML and CSS as tools as well as deliverables has become a huge part of my design workflow. I use code like I use Fireworks and I quickly iterate through design ideas by rapidly writing and rewriting CSS. I need writing code to be fast and fluid so I look out for tools that reduce friction.

Sass was a clear choice, and today I can't imagine writing CSS without it. I'd miss its extends, nested selectors, and variables. I'd miss mixins and the way Sass helps me manage color throughout my style sheets. But getting comfortable with Sass took more time than I would've liked.

That's why I wish I'd had this book when I was learning Sass. Ben has a rare talent for explaining complex concepts in clear language and he makes everything look simple and sound enjoyable. As a designer I felt Ben had written this book with me in mind and I'm sure developers will feel the same way.

I hope, no I know, that you'll enjoy this book as much as I did.

— Andrew Clarke

Andrew Clarke is a web designer at Stuff and Nonsense (`http://stuffandnonsense.co.uk`), author of the best-selling book *Transcending CSS* and the critically acclaimed *Hardboiled Web Design*, and co-host of the web business podcast Unfinished Business (`http://unfinished.bz`).

About the Author

Ben Frain has been a frontend web designer/developer since 1996. He also works as a technology journalist, contributing regularly to a number of diverse publications on the Mac platform, consumer technology, website design, and the aviation industry.

Before that, he worked as an underrated (and modest) TV actor, having graduated from Salford University with a degree in Media and Performance. He has written four equally underrated (his opinion) screenplays and still harbors the (fading) belief he might sell one. Outside of work he enjoys simple pleasures; playing indoor football while his body (and wife) still allow it, and wrestling with his son.

Visit him online at www.benfrain.com and follow him on Twitter at twitter.com/benfrain.

Thanks first and foremost to the creators, maintainers, and contributors to the Sass and Compass projects. Thanks to their combined efforts we have a brilliant tool that makes wrangling cross-browser CSS easier than ever before.

Next, I'd like to thank the technical reviewers of this book for giving up their free time to provide heaps of valuable input to make this a better product.

Finally, a note of appreciation to my family. Many episodes of sub-standard TV (wife), delicious cups of tea (parents), and piratical sword-fights (son) were sacrificed for the writing of this book.

About the Reviewers

Daniel Eden is a student, writer, designer, and developer from Manchester, UK, currently studying at Nottingham Trent University. In 2011, he created the CSS animation library, `Animate.css`, which has since been used by companies such as Hipstamatic, Foursquare, and EA Games.

Matt Mitchell is a graphic designer, who fell in love with designing for the web 10 years ago. With that came an unhealthy obsession with typography, grids, and harmony in design. He'll bore anyone who will listen about the power of musicality and proportion, never quite getting over the failure of his many musical projects. Currently head of web design at `www.bet365.com`, he has to fight the strong urge to be a designer by day and by night.

See what Matt's up to at `mattmitchell.co.uk` or on Twitter `@_m_d_m`.

Matt Wilcox is lead developer at View Creative Agency; a team of twenty-something designers, illustrators, typographers, artists, and web-developers working hard to raise the reputation of North Wales' creative sector. His role encompasses the frontend skills he's honed since starting out in the industry nine years ago and includes continual learning, sharing of ideas, teaching, project management, and meeting the unique challenges of working with a mix of clients and co-workers from differing creative backgrounds. He's sure no other group could have come up with something like our local chippie's website (`http://enochs.co.uk`) while simultaneously delivering big-name projects for world-renowned companies in both electronic and print media.

Matt is also responsible for `http://adaptive-images.com` — an early attempt to deal with the problem of image file size in a newly responsive world. He's grateful to Ben for being invited to preview this fine book (and he hopes you enjoy it as much as he has!), and for the kind words about Adaptive Images in Ben's previous book.

I'd like to thank the countless people who've given me opportunities, been inspirations, teachers, sounding-boards, and friends; I won't list names because that's just boring and irrelevant for anyone else. Some of you know who you are, others may not. If I've argued passionately with you about some minutiae of nerdy stuff, you're likely on the list.

I believe in the power of the Web and those who make it: in making and sharing for the sake of betterment; in creating amazing, passionate, and empathetic communities; and in improving the human condition through it all. High-five people of the Web; including you dear reader, for reading this book and learning more. You rock.

www.PacktPub.com

Support files, eBooks, discount offers and more

You might want to visit www.PacktPub.com for support files and downloads related to your book.

Did you know that Packt offers eBook versions of every book published, with PDF and ePub files available? You can upgrade to the eBook version at www.PacktPub.com and as a print book customer, you are entitled to a discount on the eBook copy. Get in touch with us at service@packtpub.com for more details.

At www.PacktPub.com, you can also read a collection of free technical articles, sign up for a range of free newsletters and receive exclusive discounts and offers on Packt books and eBooks.

http://PacktLib.PacktPub.com

Do you need instant solutions to your IT questions? PacktLib is Packt's online digital book library. Here, you can access, read and search across Packt's entire library of books.

Why Subscribe?

- Fully searchable across every book published by Packt
- Copy and paste, print and bookmark content
- On demand and accessible via web browser

Free Access for Packt account holders

If you have an account with Packt at www.PacktPub.com, you can use this to access PacktLib today and view nine entirely free books. Simply use your login credentials for immediate access.

Table of Contents

Preface

Do you spend your days writing CSS? If so, you need Sass and Compass in your life. It allows you to write style sheets faster, maintain them more easily, and create cutting-edge cross-browser CSS effortlessly.

Historically, getting up and running with Sass and Compass was difficult. It required an understanding of the command line and an appreciation of programming conventions.

With this book, however, we explain things in simple layman's terms. It's aimed at designers and not programmers. If you are able to understand and write HTML and CSS, with this book you will be able to master Sass and Compass and take your style sheets to the next level.

What this book covers

Chapter 1, Getting Started with Sass and Compass, explains, in layman's terms, what Sass and Compass are, how they relate, and how to get them installed and ready to use.

Chapter 2, Setting Up a Sass and Compass project, helps you get to grips with Compass projects and understand how to control them. When finished we will have a base Sass and Compass project for easy re-use.

Chapter 3, Nesting, Extend, Placeholders, and Mixins, explains the workhorse features of Sass and Compass and how they will make writing and maintaining CSS easier than ever before.

Chapter 4, Manipulate Color with Ease, allows you to kiss your color picker goodbye. With Sass and Compass it's possible to perform color conversions in the code. Saturate, mix, tint, and shade colors with ease. This chapter shows you how.

Chapter 5, Responsive and Flexible Grids with Sass and Compass, teaches how easy it is to use Sass and Compass powered grid systems to achieve any type of responsive layout without adding any extraneous HTML classes to the markup.

Chapter 6, Advanced Media Queries with Sass and Mixins, writing media queries is normally a chore. Not with Sass and Compass. This chapter explains how to generate media queries wherever you need them, giving you control of your styles on any device.

Chapter 7, Easy CSS3, Image Sprites, and More with Compass, explains how Compass makes it easy and simple to create vendor prefixes for all experimental CSS features. If that wasn't good enough, we'll use it to effortlessly create image sprites and data URIs.

Chapter 8, Programmatic Logic with Sass, covers some of the more complex but powerful features of Sass. We'll learn how to perform math functions and write loops to create countless CSS rules in a fraction of the usual time.

Chapter 9, Becoming a Sass and Compass Power User, we're almost Sass and Compass wizards now. However, in this chapter, to ensure we use our new superpowers responsibly, we'll do a code review and consider how to use development tools to test code before deployment.

What you need for this book

A good understanding of HTML and CSS is all you need.

However, familiarity with responsive web design would be beneficial and an appreciation of some great films will go a long way to your overall enjoyment of this book.

Who this book is for

Sass and Compass makes writing and maintaining CSS easier than ever before. And you don't need to be a rocket scientist to use it.

Perhaps you've heard about Sass and Compass but feel blinded by terminology. Or maybe you conceptually understand all the benefits but don't know where to start.

The book is aimed at web designers, not programmers. All you need is an understanding of HTML and CSS. With that knowledge and this book you can take your CSS skills to the next level and beyond.

Conventions

In this book, you will find a number of styles of text that distinguish between different kinds of information. Here are some examples of these styles, and an explanation of their meaning.

Code words in text, database table names, folder names, filenames, file extensions, pathnames, dummy URLs, user input, and Twitter handles are shown as follows: "Semantic purists argue that writing markup laden with HTML classes such as `column_8` and `column_4` is tantamount to a cardinal sin."

A block of code is set as follows:

```
* {
  @include bs;
}
[class^="inner"] {
  max-width: 75em;
  margin: auto;
}
header[role="banner"],footer[role="contentinfo"] {
  width: 100%;
  display: block;
}
nav[role="navigation"] {
  width: 25%;
  float: left;
}
.main-content {
  width: 70%;
  float: right;
}
footer[role="contentinfo"] {
  clear: both;
}
```

When we wish to draw your attention to a particular part of a code block, the relevant lines or items are set in bold:

```
.buy-amazon-uk {
  @extend %block;
  background-image: image-url("amazon-co-uk.png");
  background-size: image-width("amazon-co-uk.png") image-height("amazon-co-uk.png");
  background-position: 50% 50%;
  background-repeat: no-repeat;
  height: image-height("amazon-co-uk.png");
  width: image-width("amazon-co-uk.png");
}
```

Any command-line input or output is written as follows:

```
gem install susy
```

New terms and **important words** are shown in bold. Words that you see on the screen, in menus or dialog boxes for example, appear in the text like this: "The preceding example will produce an error **Cannot specify HSL and RGB values for a color at the same time for 'adjust-color'**".

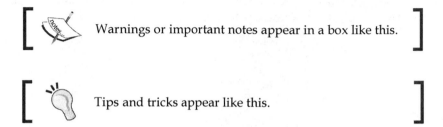

Warnings or important notes appear in a box like this.

Tips and tricks appear like this.

Reader feedback

Feedback from our readers is always welcome. Let us know what you think about this book—what you liked or may have disliked. Reader feedback is important for us to develop titles that you really get the most out of.

To send us general feedback, simply send an e-mail to feedback@packtpub.com, and mention the book title via the subject of your message.

If there is a topic that you have expertise in and you are interested in either writing or contributing to a book, see our author guide on www.packtpub.com/authors.

Customer support

Now that you are the proud owner of a Packt book, we have a number of things to help you to get the most from your purchase.

Downloading the example code

You can download the example code files for all Packt books you have purchased from your account at http://www.packtpub.com. If you purchased this book elsewhere, you can visit http://www.packtpub.com/support and register to have the files e-mailed directly to you.

Errata

Although we have taken every care to ensure the accuracy of our content, mistakes do happen. If you find a mistake in one of our books—maybe a mistake in the text or the code—we would be grateful if you would report this to us. By doing so, you can save other readers from frustration and help us improve subsequent versions of this book. If you find any errata, please report them by visiting http://www.packtpub.com/submit-errata, selecting your book, clicking on the **errata submission form** link, and entering the details of your errata. Once your errata are verified, your submission will be accepted and the errata will be uploaded on our website, or added to any list of existing errata, under the Errata section of that title. Any existing errata can be viewed by selecting your title from http://www.packtpub.com/support.

Piracy

Piracy of copyright material on the Internet is an ongoing problem across all media. At Packt, we take the protection of our copyright and licenses very seriously. If you come across any illegal copies of our works, in any form, on the Internet, please provide us with the location address or website name immediately so that we can pursue a remedy.

Please contact us at copyright@packtpub.com with a link to the suspected pirated material.

We appreciate your help in protecting our authors, and our ability to bring you valuable content.

Questions

You can contact us at questions@packtpub.com if you are having a problem with any aspect of the book, and we will do our best to address it.

1
Getting Started with Sass and Compass

Writing style sheets with Sass and Compass makes them more flexible, more maintainable, and faster to produce than ever before. That's why companies including eBay, bet365.com, BBC, Instagram, LinkedIn, Square, and Groupon all use Sass and Compass to produce their CSS.

One thing that kept me away from using Sass for too long is how difficult it seemed to get up and running. The thought of needing to use the command line to get something working made me tremble with fear, so when instructions included phrases like 'install ruby gems' and 'run the watch command', I was lost. In the words of Dr Evil, "Throw me a frickin' bone!"

If you're primarily a designer, you may have had a similar reaction. The aim of this book is to make Sass and Compass as understandable and easy to use as possible. That way all of its incredible features can be put to good use right away. I want to assure you right now that if you can write HTML and CSS you can easily master Sass and Compass.

Sass describes itself as a meta language. It's more commonly described as a CSS 'preprocessor'. Either way, the reality of using Sass is simple. Code is written as one file (a Sass file with an extension like `.scss`) and when the file is saved, Sass converts it into the same CSS you already know how to write (and if you don't know how to write CSS, put this book down and move to another shelf).

It's actually simple to make a Sass file too. Take any existing CSS file and change the file extension from `.css` to `.scss`. That is now a fully functional Sass file that you can add extra Sass based functionality to; just think of Sass as supercharged CSS.

If the command line side of things still bothers you, fear not. There are now a number of user-friendly graphical tools to make working with Sass and Compass simple. We'll cover those in this chapter (as well as using Sass and Compass from the command line for those feeling brave).

As this book is aimed at designers, after extolling the virtues of Sass and Compass, this chapter is primarily focused on understanding what Sass and Compass are, how the two relate, and then getting them both installed. Then we will be ready to start our first project.

In summary, in this chapter we will learn:

- Why CSS preprocessors are needed
- Why you should use Sass and Compass
- What Sass is
- What Compass is and how it relates to Sass
- How to install Sass and Compass on OS X and Windows
- Which graphical tools are available to negate the need to use the command line
- The different syntaxes of Sass

Why do we need CSS preprocessors?

CSS is a declarative, not a programming language. This simply means that the style properties and values that we declare within the rules of CSS are exactly what the browser uses to paint the screen. A programming language on the other hand provides some means of defining logic. Crudely put, a logical statement might be in the form of: if the h1 elements are in a nav element, make them blue; if they are in the header elements, make them red. A programming language also facilitates **variables**. These can be thought of as placeholders for something reusable (for example, one might have a variable for a specific color value). Then there are **functions**, a means to manipulate values with operations (for example, make this color 20 percent lighter). Sass and Compass provide these capabilities and more.

If some of the terminology in that last paragraph sounded alien, fear not. We will be dealing with all those concepts in due course. For now, let's just consider some common misgivings about CSS preprocessors.

If it ends up producing CSS, why not just write CSS?

My initial reaction when looking at the CSS preprocessor Sass was, 'If it ends up producing CSS, why don't I just write CSS?' Turns out, this is a reaction many people have. After all, we use CSS everyday. We can (hopefully) use it to fix all the usual layout problems that get thrown at us, build responsive websites that are displayed beautifully on all devices, and generally make ourselves feel like, for the most part, we know what we are doing.

Let's be clear from the outset. Sass won't necessarily make us produce better CSS. For example, if you don't understand how to use CSS now, Sass and Compass won't fill that gap in your knowledge. However, Sass enables us to write CSS faster and more easily while also keeping the style sheets far more maintainable.

Sass, LESS, or Stylus?

The chances are, if you are reading this, you have already done a little research and decided to look into Sass as opposed to LESS or Stylus. LESS and Stylus are also CSS preprocessors that do similar things to Sass. It is my humble opinion that Sass is a better and more powerful language, although I'll concede that the documentation for LESS in particular can make it seem easier to get to grips with. However, if you'd like to read a good summary of the various pros and cons of Sass and LESS, take a look at this great post on the *CSS Tricks* website, written by CSS maestro Chris Coyier: `http://css-tricks.com/sass-vs-less/`.

Why you should use Sass and Compass

As mentioned previously, there is a growing number of organizations such as the BBC, eBay, and LinkedIn that have already embraced Sass and Compass and use it to write and maintain their style sheets. It stands to reason that when large organizations are switching from writing CSS directly to using the Sass preprocessor there must be some enormous economies to make it worth their while. There are! So let's take a brief look at some of the headline features of using Sass now. This is by no means an exhaustive list, but hopefully it provides a tantalizing taste of what's possible and how Sass and Compass can make writing CSS easier than ever before.

Use variables (only define a value once)

How many times when you work on a website do you need to declare the value of a color in CSS? Usually as a **hex** (hexadecimal) value like #bfbfbf. 10 times? 20? However many it ends up being, I often (in fact usually) struggle to remember hex values, especially with 2-3 colors in a site. With Sass, we can just define the colors as variables. A variable is merely a mechanism for referencing a value. Take at look at these three variables:

```
$red: #ff0b13;
$blue: #091fff;
$green: #11c909;
```

Understanding the syntax of variables

The dollar sign indicates to Sass that we are defining the start of a variable. Then comes the name of the variable (with no space after the dollar sign). Then a colon indicates the end of the variable name, meaning that the value will come after the colon but before a closing semicolon. In this case, the variable $green is going to be the color of green we want as a hex value. With those colors defined as variables, we can use them anywhere in the Sass style sheet like this:

```
.i-want-to-be-green {
  color: $green;
}
```

Here is the CSS generated on compile:

```
.i-want-to-be-green {
  color: #11c909;
}
```

In Sass, **compile** just means to go from Sass to CSS.

In Sass speak, you will see the term 'compile' used frequently. For our purposes, all you need to know is that compile just means go from Sass (in either .scss or .sass format—more of which shortly) to CSS. See? Easy!

Writing and remembering variable names is far easier than remembering unnatural hex values, no? Furthermore, when those color values need to change, they only need changing at the variable and everywhere else takes care of itself. No more 'find and replace' when the colors in a design change—Woo Hoo!

Automatic RGBA color values and conversions

RGBA (Red Green Blue Alpha) and **HSLA (Hue Saturation Lightness Alpha)** colors are supported increasingly in modern browsers. To provide a fallback for older browsers it's common to declare a hex color value first and then an RGBA or HSLA value for newer browsers (that way, new browsers use the RGBA/HSLA, while older ones use the solid hex value). To exemplify that technique, to enable a color with some alpha transparency, at present we might do this:

```
.color-me-bad {
  color: #11c909;
  color: rgba(17, 201, 9, 0.9);
}
```

If picking colors from a composite in a graphics application (Photoshop, Fireworks, and the like), it is not always simple to get both hex and RGBA values. Before Sass, I had a handy little application just for the job. Now, I am pleased to say that thanks to Sass, that application has gone the way of the Dodo. With Sass, it is possible to simply do this:

```
.color-me-good {
  color: $green;
  color: rgba($green, 0.9);
}
```

We're using an easy to remember variable name to represent the color and then using a color function of Sass to convert that color to RGBA. In the preceding example we are asking Sass to give the value of the color (defined as the `$green` variable) as an RGBA value with an alpha channel at 0.9. When compiled, it produces the following CSS code:

```
.color-me-good {
  color: #11c909;
  color: rgba(17, 201, 9, 0.9);
}
```

For those in the cheap seats not paying attention, Sass has automatically provided the color as an RGBA value. The alpha channel is at 90 percent. This means that we can see 10 percent of whatever is behind the color in browsers that understand RGBA.

Forget about vendor prefixes

I'm a big fan of CSS3. It lets us ditch images and do more things with pure CSS than ever before. However, implementing these new features (background gradients, box-shadows, transformations, and a few more), that are often still experimental features, often requires the use of vendor prefixes and occasionally different syntaxes. You know the drill. As an example, this is what historically has been needed for rounded corners:

```
.rounded {
 -webkit-border-radius: 4px;
 -moz-border-radius: 4px;
 -ms-border-radius: 4px;
 -o-border-radius: 4px;
 border-radius: 4px;
}
```

With Sass's authoring framework, Compass, we get heaps of free **mixins** (don't worry about what a mixin actually is, we'll get to that shortly). Instead of remembering prefixes and associated syntaxes, you can just write the following code:

```
.rounded {
  @include border-radius(4px);
}
```

And that would produce exactly the same CSS on compile; all of the vendor prefixes get automatically generated. It's a huge time saver.

Nesting rules

Sass allows rules to be nested within one another. So for example, if you wanted to make a set of links with a nav element and provide alternative pseudo states for hover and active states, you could write this in Sass:

```
nav {
  a {
    color: $red;
    &:hover {
      color: $green;
    }
    &:visited {
      color: $blue;
    }
  }
}
```

We are putting the anchor links (the a tag) within the nav element and also nesting the hover tag and visited states within the a tag. This probably looks more complicated than it actually is. Here's how that compiles to CSS:

```
nav a {
  color: #ff0b13;
}
nav a:hover {
  color: #11c909;
}
nav a:visited {
  color: #091fff;
}
```

I like to do this on little self-contained modules of CSS as it keeps all the associated styles together, especially where pseudo classes (like :hover and :active) are needed.

Keep in mind that it's rarely good practice when writing CSS selectors to make them too specific. For instance, here is an example of the kind of CSS rule that can make life difficult:

```
#container .callout-area ul#callout-one li.callout-list a.callout-link {
  color: #bfbfbf;
}
```

The resultant selector is many levels deep, making it very specific. From a maintainability point of view it would be far easier to simply have this to achieve the same effect:

```
.callout-link {
  color: #bfbfbf;
}
```

So, keep in mind that just because you can nest rules doesn't mean you always should.

Media queries the simple way

Unless there is a good reason not to, I believe all websites should be built responsively (cough, buy my book *Responsive web design with HTML5 and CSS3*). In CSS terms, this typically involves writing lots of media queries for the different **breakpoints** in a design. For example, to change the typography at a certain viewport/device width you might write this CSS:

```
@media only screen and (min-width: 280px) and (max-width: 479px) {
  .h1 {
    font-size: 1.1em;
  }
}
@media only screen and (min-width: 480px) and (max-width: 599px) {
  .h1 {
    font-size: 1em;
  }
}
@media only screen and (min-width: 600px) and (max-width: 767px) {
  .h1 {
    font-size: 0.9em;
  }
}
```

That code sets a different font size on the h1 element depending upon the screen width in pixels. Personally, I think this is quite verbose and a lot to remember.

With Sass, instead, it is possible to do this:

```
h1 {
  @include MQ(XS) {
    font-size: 1.1em;
  }
  @include MQ(S) {
    font-size: 1em;
  }
  @include MQ(M) {
    font-size: 0.9em;
  }
}
```

A variable is defined for XS, S and M elsewhere (each is just a width value). The value of the variable is then used inside a mixin called MQ. Using that MQ mixin, media queries can be placed easily wherever they are needed, arguably making it simpler to understand where they are being applied in the code.

Automatic compression of CSS for faster websites

I've talked about some of the compelling features of Sass and Compass and not even mentioned @extend, placeholder styles, partial files, or image sprites; I hope you'll stick around for later chapters when we get into using them. In the meantime, as Columbo and Steve Jobs would say, 'Just one more thing...'.

How do you compress CSS before using it on a live site? Compressing the CSS makes it a fraction of its original size, resulting in faster code for every device that requests it. Compressing CSS can easily reduce the file size by half its original uncompressed size. Sure it's possible to copy and paste the CSS into an online compression tool, or perhaps your text editor has a built-in feature for the task, but Sass is better still. It just does it.

Sass can be configured to compile the CSS in a number of formats, one of which is compressed. So as soon as the Sass file is saved, it gets automatically compiled into compressed CSS; production ready and in the smallest possible file size. A time saver and something every user of the sites you build will benefit from, even if they don't know it.

So that's it; I've given you a few brief nuggets of what Sass and Compass can do. Next, let's get a handle on what Sass and Compass actually are and then we'll get up and running.

What is Sass?

The website of Sass (http://sass-lang.com/) makes this description of Sass:

> *Sass is a meta-language on top of CSS that's used to describe the style of a document cleanly and structurally, with more power than flat CSS allows. Sass both provides a simpler, more elegant syntax for CSS and implements various features that are useful for creating manageable style sheets.*

The Sass website also provides some insight in to how Sass came about and developed. Sass was first given life by Hampton Catlin (also the creator of **HAML**) in 2006. Since then, it has been fostered, loved, and cared for by a number of others. However, most notable in the development of Sass is Nathan Weizembaum (the primary designer and developer who developed Sass with Hampton Catlin until Version 2) and Christopher Eppstein (who joined Weizembaum on the Sass core team in 2008 and developed the project with him from Version 2.2 onwards. Eppstein is also the creator of the Compass framework). There are also a number of other contributors to the Sass project. The project's GitHub development homepage can be found at http://github.com/nex3/sass.

As Sass started life in the Ruby community (Ruby is itself a programming language), much of the documentation associated with Sass has always been programmer friendly. Historically, this has made Sass difficult for non-programmers to get their heads around. This is a great shame, as designers who also write their own frontend code arguably stand to benefit as much as anyone else from its power and features.

Sass also supports two syntaxes. The original syntax (known as Sass, with files ending in a .sass extension) is terse and based on indentation. It removes the curly braces we're used to seeing in CSS. You can find more documentation on the indented syntax at http://sass-lang.com/docs/yardoc/file.INDENTED_ SYNTAX.html.

The syntax we will be using throughout this book is the SCSS based syntax, with Sass files ending in the .scss extension. This syntax is more verbose than the original indent-based syntax but similar to existing CSS.

Wynn Netherland, Nathan Weizembaum, and Christopher Eppstein have their own book on Sass and Compass, *Sass and Compass in Action*. As Nathan Weizembaum and Christopher Eppstein are the current maintainers of Sass, while the title isn't specifically targeted at designers, it may be worth your attention. Take a look at http://manning.com/netherland/.

Sass is free to use, requiring no license.

What is Compass?

The Compass website is at `http://compass-style.org`. It describes itself as follows:

> *Compass is an open-source CSS Authoring Framework.*

In fact, Compass was the first Sass-based framework. What this boils down to is that by installing Compass alongside Sass we get access to lots and lots of reusable patterns and tools for easily creating CSS. Have you seen the TV show *Pimp my ride*? If Xzibit took Sass into West Coast Customs, Compass would be the first thing they added!

Put another way, Compass lets you write CSS3 goodies like box-shadow, gradients, columns, and transforms with a single syntax, and it magically creates cross-browser compatible CSS of everything that just works without headaches. It also paves the way for additional plugins to enable incredible, lightweight grid systems that we will be looking at in due course.

The project's GitHub development homepage can be found at `https://github.com/chriseppstein/compass`.

Compass is **charityware**. This means that while you can use it as much as you like, you are encouraged to make a donation to help the UMDF find a cure for mitochondrial disease. Once you use Compass and realize how much time it saves, I'd encourage you to make a donation at `http://umdf.org/compass/`.

Install Sass and Compass

In days gone by, to use Sass and Compass, it was necessary to use the command line to install them. Don't worry, those days are over. If you're not a fan of the command line, you don't have to use it. There are now a number of graphical tools for OS X, Linux, and Windows that will include all the necessary files to compile Sass files to CSS whenever they are saved. However, while we'll look at these tools, we can totally install Sass and Compass from the command line. Are you ready? Let's do this.

If you'd rather not, I understand, just skip ahead to the section on graphical tools. You can always come back here later. I won't judge!

Install the package for OS X

For those using Mac OS X, it is really simple to install Sass and Compass. Compass creator Chris Eppstein has created a graphical installer package. Just head to `https://github.com/chriseppstein/compass/downloads`, download the package, and run the latest installer.

However, understanding just a little about the command line will be beneficial, so you may opt to flex your command line muscles just a little and install from there.

> **Getting around on the command line**
>
> There are only a few commands that are essential to work with Sass and Compass on the command line. Following are the ones you'll probably need to know:
>
> List the items in the current folder:
>
> Windows:
> `dir`
>
> Mac:
> `ls`
>
> Change directory/folder — moving to another folder within the current one:
>
> Windows and Mac:
>
> `cd folder-name`
>
> Here `folder-name` is the name of the folder you want to change to
>
> To move to the parent folder:
>
> Windows:
> `cd..`
>
> Mac
> `cd ..`

Installing and working with Sass and Compass on the command line

Before we can install Sass and Compass, we need Ruby installed. If you are on OS X, you already have it.

Installing Ruby on Windows

If you are on Windows, head over to `http://rubyinstaller.org/downloads/`, download, and install the latest Ruby installer file (for example, it will be a file link as follows, depending upon the current version: `http://rubyforge.org/frs/download.php/76054/rubyinstaller-1.9.3-p194.exe`). Just use the defaults (you don't need to put any tick boxes in the options). Linux users should be able to install Ruby direct from their package manager.

I'm assuming if you are running Linux you are savvy enough to understand what to do, if not, I'd suggest getting a Mac!

Running a gem command

Now, regardless of the system (Windows/Linux/Mac), we have Ruby ready. We're going to use the Ruby `gem` command. Basically, we are just saying, "Ruby, install me the 'gem' called 'compass'". Compass actually requires Sass, so by installing Compass, Ruby will automatically install Sass too.

> Think of a **gem** as a tiny application or plugin; it simply extends the functionality of something that uses Ruby. Because Sass and Compass use Ruby, once you get into Sass, you'll often find yourself downloading new gems. For example, there are gems for grid systems like Susy, gems for button styles like Sassy Buttons, and lots, lots more.

Mac OS X command line install

Those on OS X should open the Terminal application. It's typically located in the **Applications | Utilities** folder. Here's the Terminal application in my Finder:

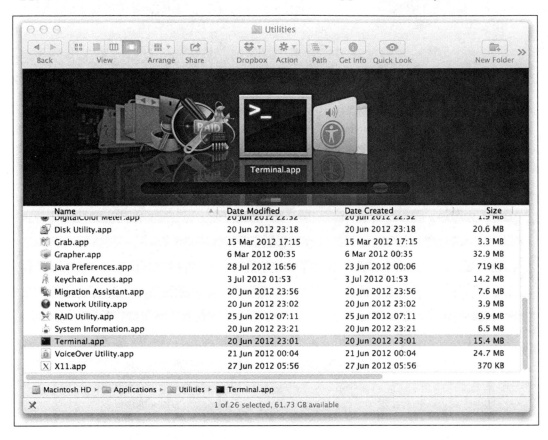

Double-click on that and you'll see a window like the following screenshot:

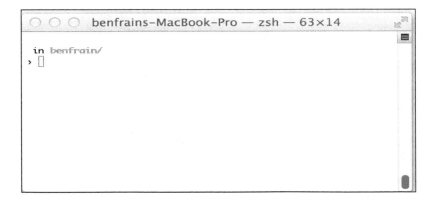

In case you've never been here before, this is the command line! Now just type this and then press *Enter*:

```
sudo gem install compass
```

You will be prompted for your user password (it's the same one you use to log into your desktop). Just type it in and press *Enter*. Don't be alarmed when it seems that nothing is happening. When entering a password, the Terminal provides no feedback. With that done, Compass and Sass will install.

How about that, you just installed a Ruby gem. Do you feel like a nerd now? Don't worry, it'll be our little secret.

Windows command prompt install

For Windows users using Windows 7 or Vista, just click on the Start button and type `ruby`, and then click on the highlighted **Start Command Prompt with Ruby** option. Those on Windows 8, from the **Start** screen, right-click, choose **All apps,** and then click on the **Start Command Prompt with Ruby** option.

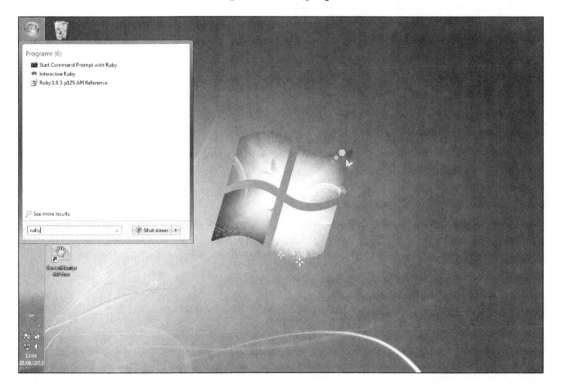

The Command Prompt will now open as shown in the following screenshot:

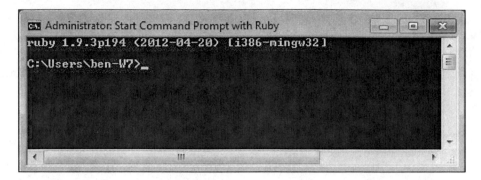

Just type the following command and press *Enter*:

```
gem install compass
```

Compass and Sass will now install, and when finished you will be presented with another Command Prompt (a blinking cursor).

There, that's all there is to it. Sass and Compass are installed; you can now start writing Sass and Compass files.

Check which version of Sass and Compass you have

As new features get added to Sass and Compass from time to time, it's worth knowing how to check your current version and install the latest versions. Check the current version of Sass from the command line with the following command:

```
sass -v
```

You will see a response, something like `Sass 3.2.5 (Media Mark)`.

To check the current version of compass, run the following command:

```
compass -v
```

You will get a response on the command line such as `Compass 0.12.2 (Alnilam)`.

 In case you are wondering, Alnilam is the middle star in the belt of Orion (yes, I Googled it).

Check which versions of Sass and Compass are available

Of course, it's possible to check the websites of Sass and Compass to find out which versions of each are available, but this can also be done from the command line. Just run the following command:

```
gem list sass -a -r
```

We are just asking Ruby to list the versions of all the gems that have sass in their name. The -r part of the command is asking Ruby to check remotely (for example, on the Internet as opposed to on your own system) and the -a part is just asking Ruby to list all the versions. Here's the same command for Compass:

```
gem list compass -a -r
```

With either of those commands, you'll get a list of all the gems that contain the word Sass or Compass respectively, with the version numbers listed in brackets. For example:

```
sass (3.2.0, 3.1.21, 3.1.20, 3.1.19, 3.1.18, 3.1.17, 3.1.16, 3.1.15,
3.1.14, 3.1.13, 3.1.12, 3.1.11, 3.1.10, 3.1.9, 3.1.8, 3.1.7, 3.1.6,
3.1.5, 3.1.4, 3.1.3, 3.1.2, 3.1.1, 3.1.0)
```

The versions are listed in reverse chronological order (latest first).

To check which prerelease versions are available, the command is:

```
gem list sass --pre -r
```

To check which prerelease versions of Compass are available, the command is as follows:

```
gem list compass --pre -r
```

Installing the latest version of Sass and Compass (including prerelease versions)

To install the latest stable version of Sass, just run the following command (the sudo part may not be needed depending upon your system configuration):

```
sudo gem install sass
```

If a future version has something exciting you want to try out but it isn't yet a full stable release, you can install the latest prerelease version by running this command:

```
sudo gem install sass --pre
```

However, be aware that there may be bugs and inconsistencies with the latest version. So, unless you have a specific reason to do so, I'd recommend only using the stable versions.

It's the same style of command for Compass:

```
sudo gem install compass
```

And for the prerelease version:

```
sudo gem install compass -pre
```

How to uninstall a specific version of Sass

Now, should things go pear-shaped at any point, you can roll back to a previous version of Sass by using the following command:

```
gem uninstall sass --version versionnumber
```

Here, versionnumber is the release you want to remove (for example, 3.2.0.alpha.103).

Create a Sass and Compass project from the command line

Want to create a Sass and Compass project from the command line? This can be done by changing folders in the command line to where the site folder should be (for example, I tend to keep mine in a folder called Sites) and running this command:

```
compass create my-project
```

Hopefully that command is self-explanatory; we're just using Compass's built-in create command to make a project in the folder specified. For example, the my-project part is the name of the project folder that will be created. Compass then creates a number of files and folders. Following is an example of the resultant files in Windows:

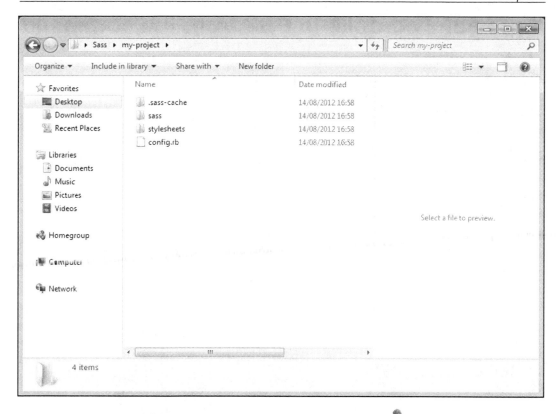

What are the generated files in a Compass project for?

We'll cover what the various files and folders do in depth in *Chapter 2, Setting Up a Sass and Compass project*. In the meantime, here's a quick overview of what each does:

.sass-cache: This folder will contain the cache files that Sass uses to build your CSS files faster. You don't need to do anything with it.

sass: This folder will store the Sass files that will be written or amended. This folder can be called anything, but 'sass' is the default name.

stylesheets: This folder will contain the compiled CSS files that Sass will generate. It can be called anything, but stylesheets is the default folder name in Compass projects.

config.rb: This file contains the configuration defaults for a project, what the various folders are called, and where they are located. It also controls the compression style of the generated CSS.

Automatic compile to CSS from the command line

To have Compass 'watch' the Sass files for changes (which are in the `sass` folder of the project) and automatically compile them into CSS on save, it's necessary to first browse to the folder that holds the Sass files being worked on (it may help to refer back to the *Getting around on the command line* tip box in the *Install Sass and Compass* section for the relevant commands). When at the root of the relevant folder (when listing the contents of the folder you are in, the `config.rb` file should be listed) run this command from the command line:

```
compass watch
```

This Compass command just says "Compass, watch this project, and if any Sass files change, recompile the CSS". Now, whenever the Sass files within are changed, Compass will automatically note any changes and recompile the equivalent CSS files (the CSS is compiled into the `stylesheets` folder of a Compass project by default).

Graphical tools for working with Sass and Compass

There are a number of graphical tools that handle all of this Ruby gem shenanigan business (they all include their own versions of Ruby) and compile Sass files into CSS. The three we will look at are **LiveReload** (OS X and Windows), **CodeKit** (OS X only), and **Scout** (OS X and Windows).

I initially used the command line to work with Sass and Compass, but nowadays, unless there are specific commands I need to run, I tend to use LiveReload or CodeKit day-to-day. However, there is no right tool to use. Just use the one that works best for you.

Whichever you choose, in a few clicks, all the business of watching files for changes is handled automatically. Just ensure the application is running and get on with writing Sass files.

Scout app

Scout is a free Adobe Air-based application. It can be downloaded at `http://mhs.github.com/scout-app`. Once installed, run the application and click on the big plus button at the bottom left of the interface to add a project. It's still necessary to configure the settings, but once done the compile process will be automated. It's free, but personally I think it's worth investing a little money on one of the other solutions (described next) as they offer extra functionality that can soon pay for itself.

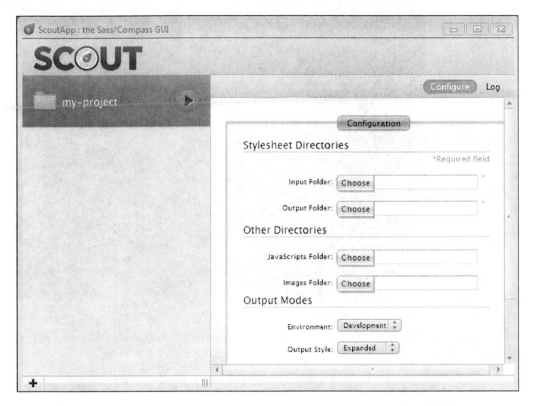

CodeKit

CodeKit is a Mac OS X only application (sorry Windows and Linux folks). It has a great, simple user interface and not only compiles Sass files (along with a bunch of other preprocessor languages), it also reloads the browser window as files are saved; a real timesaver when iterating over styles. It can also concatenate files and a whole lot more.

What is particularly nice about CodeKit is that it gives the option to create Compass projects directly from the interface. Just specify the preferences, choose a folder, and it does the rest (and then automatically watches the project for changes).

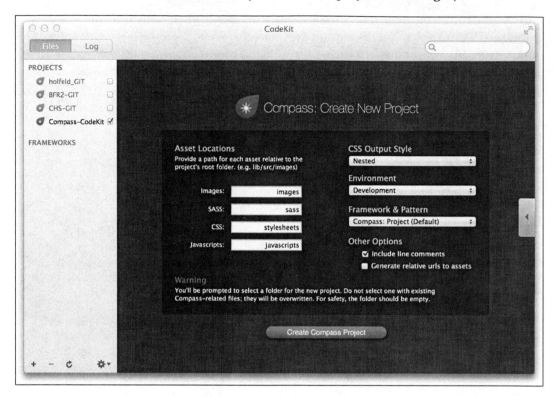

The full version is $25, but there's a free, time-limited trial, so take a look and see if it works for you: http://incident57.com/codekit/.

LiveReload

LiveReload is similar to CodeKit, in that alongside automatically compiling preprocessor languages such as Sass, it also automatically refreshes the browser window as changes to web-related files are made. Just press the plus icon at the bottom of the interface, browse to the project folder, and then tick the **Compile SASS, LESS, Stylus, CoffeeScript and others** option.

It costs $9.99 (available to OS X users through the App Store). Alongside the OS X version there is also a prerelease version available for Windows. Take a look at `http://livereload.com`.

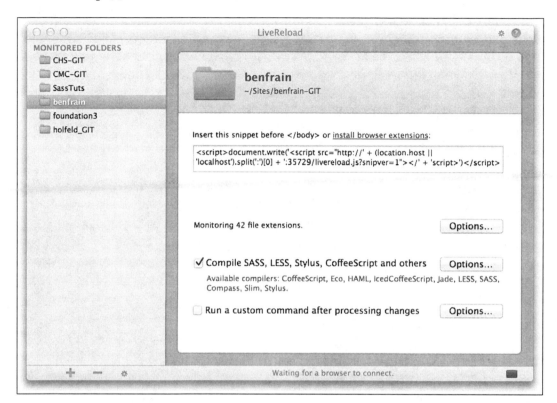

Create your first Sass file in under ten seconds

Remember, any existing CSS file can be easily converted into Sass files. Open any of your existing web projects and change the extension on a CSS file from `.css` to `.scss`. That file is now a fully working and valid Sass file.

How to work with Sass files in text editors

Text editors are like sports teams; everyone has their favorite. There isn't a right or wrong text editor to use with Sass. However, using one that supports the Sass syntax will obviously be beneficial as it will provide lovely syntax highlighting that makes the files easier to work with.

Thankfully, most quality text editors either support Sass syntax out of the box or have third-party plugins that extend the functionality to include syntax highlighting for Sass. At the time of writing this, my current text editing application of choice is Sublime Text (cross platform, available at http://sublimetext.com), although programs like Coda 2 (OS X only, available at http://panic.com/coda), Espresso 2 (OS X only, available at http://macrabbit.com), and Aptana (cross platform, available at http://aptana.com) also have native support for Sass.

Summary

In this chapter, we have looked at a few reasons to use Sass and Compass. We have also considered exactly what each is, does, and how the two relate to one another.

Then we've either installed Sass and Compass from the command line (and wrapped our heads around what Ruby gems are) or opted to use any one of the growing number of graphical tools that support Sass and Compass. Either way, we now have some mechanism in place to watch our Sass files and automatically create CSS files whenever they are saved.

Hopefully one of the biggest hurdles, getting Sass and Compass set up, is now dealt with. We can now get on with starting our first Sass and Compass project. That is exactly what we will be doing in the next chapter. We will learn all about how to amend the configuration file, the various ways we can comment Sass files, make use of partial files, and use variables for cleaner and more maintainable style sheet authoring.

2
Setting Up a Sass and Compass project

In the last chapter, *Getting Started with Sass and Compass*, we learnt about what Sass and Compass are, some of their benefits, and how to get them both installed.

In this chapter, we're going to press on and set up our first Sass and Compass project. Once we've completed this chapter, we will have a base project we can reuse every time we need to start a new web project, with everything set to our preference. It's just the start of having a more maintainable code base for future projects.

Before we get into this, indulge me a brief digression.

Have you seen the film Karate Kid (I'm talking about the 1984 original, not the new fangled remake)? In it, karate student Daniel-san wonders why he's been made to wax a car all day long for his master, Mr Miyagi, instead of being taught karate.

Mr. Miyagi reveals that the day of polishing the car a certain way (the whole 'wax-on', 'wax-off' thing) has actually taught him the most important and indispensible karate techniques.

The point I'm making is that once mastered, tasks that seem mundane and boring can often be the most important.

I'm hoping in due course you will enjoy a similar realization regarding the topics we'll cover in this chapter. They aren't what I would call the 'wow' tools and techniques of Sass and Compass, but they are essential. Furthermore, once this is done, it is unlikely that the steps will need to be repeated. Future projects will be better organized and easier to start working with.

By the way, I'm not implying I'm a master here either; closest I come is a similar hair and waistline to Mr. Miyagi.

In summary, in this chapter we will learn:

- How to create a Sass and Compass project from the command line
- How to configure Compass projects
- How to understand and tweak the Compass configuration file
- How to change the format of the CSS that is generated
- What partial files are, and how we can make them and import them into other files
- How to make a CSS reset or normalize partial file
- How to create Sass variables, store, and reuse them
- The different types of comments that can be used in Sass
- How to save a 'base' project for easy re-use

Setting up a Sass and Compass project

The whole point of using Sass and Compass for projects is to make things easier. It seems sensible therefore, that we should apply this same thinking to how we make and remake the base for each project.

Perhaps at present, when starting a new web project, a new folder is created to house the project files. Inside there, extra folders are made for CSS, JavaScript, images, and the like. Then any files that are usually used are copied over or created from scratch. Perhaps an `index.html` page, a `styles.css` in the `css` folder, and `plugins.js` and `main.js` files for the JavaScript.

We are not going to reinvent the wheel. Our final project structure will be very similar. However, we are going make things a little easier when working with Sass and Compass in the future. In the next few pages, we will set up a base project for easy reuse. This will mean it won't usually be necessary to use the command line to create new Sass and Compass projects in the future.

Automation tools for frontend development

There are a growing number of free frontend tools available to speed up web development. If you are interested in automating more of your workflow and don't fear the command line, take a look at **Yeoman** (http://yeoman.io). It not only compiles Sass for you, it also optimizes images, refreshes the browser, and has a full build system for going from development to production.

Bower (https://github.com/twitter/bower) is a little easier to get to grips with. It is a package manager from the Twitter development team, created for easily adding CSS, JavaScripts, and more to a project.

There are also a growing number of static site generators that perform similar tasks, **Middleman** being a personal favorite. Take a look at http://middlemanapp.com.

Creating Compass projects

Let's start with a blank Compass project (when using Compass alongside Sass, Compass becomes a hub for many settings and features) and then amend it to our will.

GUI tools often have buttons to create new Compass projects. For example, CodeKit has an option called **Create new Compass project**.

If not using a GUI application, it's possible to create a Compass project with the default settings from the command line. Let's do that now. Open the command line / Command Prompt (if running Windows, remember to use the Command Prompt with the Ruby option), move to the folder that should contain the project, and type this in the command line:

```
compass create
```

This will create a Compass project with a number of the default options.

Remember, the basic commands needed to get around on the command line are covered in *Chapter 1, Getting Started with Sass and Compass*.

There are other options available when creating a Compass project from the command line. Let's look at these now.

Creating a customized Compass project

It is possible to customize the folder names for different project assets (style sheets, JavaScript, images) that are created when creating a project from the command line. Simply amend the command by adding some additional parameters as follows:

```
compass create --sass-dir "sass" --css-dir "css" --javascripts-dir "js"
--images-dir "img"
```

Here, we are just telling Compass the explicit names we would like for each folder in the project. Just amend the value in the quotation marks to whatever is needed. This merely saves renaming folders after they have been created and then amending the `config.rb` file (don't worry, we'll get to the `config.rb` file in a moment).

Don't worry if it goes horribly wrong, just delete the folders the command has created and run the command again.

> It's not necessary to delete files created with the command line from the command line. For ease, just use the normal desktop GUI tools such as the Finder (OS X) or file explorer (Windows).

Once the prior command has run, there is now a folder for the style sheets (`stylesheets` by default but I've called mine `css`) with default files within (ie.`css`, `print.css` and `styles.css`), a folder for the Sass files (`sass` by default and I have kept that name) including the associated `ie.scss`, `print.scss` and `styles.scss` files, a folder for images (`images` by default but I've renamed mine to `img`) and a hidden folder called `.sass-cache`.

As mentioned in *Chapter 1, Getting Started with Sass and Compass*, the `.sass-cache` folder is a temporary storage area that Sass uses to build the CSS it generates.

> It's not necessary to touch the `.sass-cache` folder and we won't concern ourselves with it now. However, *Chapter 9, Becoming a Sass and Compass Power User*, details how to clear the Sass cache and also force compiles if you ever need to.

The Compass `create` command won't, by default, create the folder for JavaScript files, so it needs to be created manually. Either create that folder using GUI tools, or if the command line is open, do the following:

- If using Mac OS X, run this command and press *Enter*:

  ```
  mkdir js
  ```

- If using Windows, type this and press *Enter*:

```
md js
```

Now, delete the `print.scss`, `styles.scss` and `ie.scss` files from the `sass` folder and the `print.css`, `styles.css` and `ie.css` files from the `css` folder; we won't be needing those.

If creating folders and files only to delete them seems a little backward, read on.

Creating a bare Compass project

Personally, I rarely use the default `print`, `ie`, and `styles` files that Compass creates, so when creating a blank base for my projects, I add an additional parameter to my Compass `create` command:

```
compass create --bare --sass-dir "sass" --css-dir "css" --javascripts-dir "js" --images-dir "img"
```

The `--bare` parameter just prevents Compass creating and adding those initial files and folders. The only thing it will create is a `config.rb` file and a `sass` folder. If that's the case, you may be wondering why bother adding the parameters for JavaScript, CSS, and the like in the command?

Well, open the `config.rb` file in a text editor and you will see why; it includes the paths to these folders, ready to roll. Again, it's just a little time saver.

If this way sounds preferable, just ensure folders are made for `img`, `js`, and `css` (or whatever you want them to be called). Sass will automatically make the `.sass-cache` folder.

Look like a cone-headed genius!

As we are getting used to the command line, if you are running OS X, how about running a single command to create the `js` `css` and `img` folders plus a blank `index.html` page and a blank `main.js` and `plugins.js` file in the `js` folder?

At the command line, move to the root of the project folder, enter this command, and press *Enter*:

```
mkdir img js css ; touch index.html js/main.js js/plugins.js
```

How about that? We just made all those files and folders with a single command! A pinprick in the heart of all the backend savants that mock our Terminal knowledge!

From this point on, I'm going to be referring to the various folders as I have named them previously, so you'll need to keep that in mind. For an easier life, do yourself a favor and name yours the same (as you'll have enough to remember). Once you've finished the book you can call them what you want!

Before proceeding, in the root of the project there should be at least:

- A folder called `img` (probably empty)
- A folder called `js` (probably empty)
- A folder called `css` (preferably empty)
- A folder called `sass` (preferably empty)
- A file called `config.rb`

The following screenshot shows the basic structure in the OS X Finder (obviously expect a similar structure if using Windows) plus the `index.html` file we will be adding shortly:

Understanding the config.rb file

The `config.rb` file is the *brain* of a Compass project. It defines the relationship between files and their assets, how and where the CSS should be generated, and any dependencies for a project. Open the `config.rb` file in a text editor. The contents should look something like this:

Downloading the example code

You can download the example code files for all Packt books you have purchased from your account at http://www.packtpub.com. If you purchased this book elsewhere, you can visit http://www.packtpub.com/support and register to have the files e-mailed directly to you.

```
# Require any additional compass plugins here.

# Set this to the root of your project when deployed:
http_path = "/"
css_dir = "css"
sass_dir = "sass"
images_dir = "img"
javascripts_dir = "js"

# You can select your preferred output style here (can be overridden
via the command line):
# output_style = :expanded or :nested or :compact or :compressed

# To enable relative paths to assets via compass helper functions.
Uncomment:
# relative_assets = true

# To disable debugging comments that display the original location of
your selectors. Uncomment:
# line_comments = false
```

There are some other lines below the content listed above, but they are only relevant if using the indented syntax of Sass. We won't be using the indented syntax here so I have omitted those lines for brevity. However, you can leave them in the `config. rb`. Trust me, they won't do any harm!

Let's break this `config.rb` file down so we know exactly what it does and how it can help us.

When making changes to the `config.rb` file, particularly output style, it's sometimes necessary to clear the `.sass-cache` before expected changes will be seen. In this instance, either manually delete the `sass-cache` folder and it will be recreated next time a Sass file is saved, or run the following command from the command line:

`compass clean`

If using the command line to watch the project for changes, remember to start watching for changes again by running the following command:

`compass watch`

Adding the required plugins

Remember when we mentioned Ruby gems in the last chapter? There are gems for things like fancy buttons, flexible grids, boilerplate frameworks, and lots, lots more. We'll deal with some of these in later chapters. For now, all that's essential to know is that if it's necessary to reference an additional Compass plugin for a project, this is done in the config.rb file.

The first section of the config.rb file has this commented line:

```
# Require any additional compass plugins here.
```

This placeholder text provides a sensible space to specify any required plugins for the project. For example, if a project requires the use of the Susy Compass plugin (the fantastic grid system we will be looking at in depth in *Chapter 5, Responsive and Flexible Grids with Sass and Compass*), we would add this line:

```
require "susy"
```

Any required plugins can be added in this manner, typically one after another on separate lines. For now, we don't need to add anything, so let's consider what's next.

Setting the names and paths for project assets

When we created the project, we set the various folder names for assets:

```
# Set this to the root of your project when deployed:
http_path = "/"
css_dir = "css"
sass_dir = "sass"
images_dir = "img"
javascripts_dir = "js"
```

After creating a project, the path and name values in the config.rb can be amended to suit. For example, if creating a Wordpress theme, a Sass folder might be in the project root, but the CSS, images, and JavaScripts folders might be buried in a number of other folders relevant to the theme structure. For example, it might look like this:

```
http_path = "/"
css_dir = "wp-content/themes/retlehs-roots-0e51e90/css"
sass_dir = "sass"
images_dir = "wp-content/themes/retlehs-roots-0e51e90/img"
javascripts_dir = "wp-content/themes/retlehs-roots-0e51e90/js"
```

Hopefully these paths make sense; they are each relative to the HTTP path. So as long as that remains at the root (designated the root by the / symbol) the other folders are relative to it.

The default `config.rb` file made by the `compass create` command also omits another relative path that can be useful, and that's the one for web fonts. Therefore, after the other paths you may want to add this line:

```
fonts_dir= "css/fonts"
```

That way, if a project requires any web fonts, they can be stored in a `fonts` folder within the `css` folder. Obviously this is entirely optional and the path and name of the folder can be amended to suit.

Setting the CSS output style

The next section of the `config.rb` file provides options for how the compiled CSS should be output:

```
# You can select your preferred output style here (can be overridden
via the command line):
# output_style = :expanded or :nested or :compact or :compressed
```

If you don't set an output style, Sass and Compass produce rules in this format:

```
/* line 8, ../sass/styles.scss */
#main {
  color: #999;
}
/* line 10, ../sass/styles.scss */
#main .content {
  color: #bfbfbf;
}
```

There's nothing wrong with that. However, there are other options that may be preferred.

The nested output option

Sass offers an option to show the CSS nested. For example, perhaps there is a `div` element in the markup with an ID of `main` and within that a `div` element with a class of `content`. As we've seen, in Sass it's possible to nest styles to match how styles relate to one another in terms of markup structure. Therefore, in Sass, we might write rules for these elements as follows:

```
#main {
  color: #999;
  .content {
    color: #bfbfbf;
  }
}
```

If we changed the `config.rb` style to output nested styles instead by adding this line:

```
# output_style = :expanded or :nested or :compact or :compressed
output_style = :nested
```

it would produce CSS as follows:

```
/* line 8, ../sass/styles.scss */
#main {
  color: #999; }
  /* line 10, ../sass/styles.scss */
  #main .content {
    color: #bfbfbf; }
```

Can you see how the second rule is indented in the output CSS? The level of indentation mirrors the number of levels deep the rule is nested within others; it helps tie up the structure of the markup with the related styles. Personally, I never use this option, but that doesn't mean it might not be useful for you.

The compact output option

For those that are fans of the single line CSS format, this is the output option for you. Alter the `config.rb` file to have the compact output style set:

```
# output_style = :expanded or :nested or :compact or :compressed
output_style = :compact
```

Now, the same rules we produced previously will be formatted as follows:

```
/* line 8, ../sass/styles.scss */
#main { color: #999; }
/* line 10, ../sass/styles.scss */
#main .content { color: #bfbfbf; }
```

So much of CSS formatting is preference. If this output format doesn't tickle your fancy, there are other options.

The compressed output option

The compressed output option removes standard Sass and CSS comments and whitespace. It's the setting to use when you want to produce production ready code. Set it as follows in the `config.rb` file:

```
# output_style = :expanded or :nested or :compact or :compressed
output_style = :compressed
```

And this will output those same CSS rules as follows:

```
#main{color:#999}#main .content{color:#bfbfbf}
```

When starting with Sass and Compass it's normal to keep checking the CSS code that is produced. Therefore, to begin with, choose an output format that most closely resembles how you would handwrite CSS. That way it will be more understandable and legible.

It's likely that in time, you won't actually write CSS. Instead you'll be writing Sass. When that's the case, just set the output format to compressed and know that the output CSS is production ready from the outset.

Remember, you won't be reading the CSS, a browser will, so we can concentrate on making our Sass files, (the files we will actually be reading and writing), as legible as possible, and give the browser the smallest possible CSS file to serve to our users.

Remove the comments, keep the style

You may have noticed that on all but the `compressed` output option, the resultant CSS includes comments above each rule. This indicates where in the source Sass files the rule was generated. Some tools use this for debugging, allowing you to pinpoint which part a Sass file actually created that rule.

To keep one of the other output styles but remove those comments, adjust the following part of the `config.rb` file:

```
# To disable debugging comments that display the original location of
your selectors. Uncomment:
line_comments = false
```

Now, if we chose the output style of `compact`, we'd get the single line look without the comments:

```
#main { color: #999; }
#main .content { color: #bfbfbf; }
```

Compress the CSS, keep the comments (loud comments)

There may be instances when compressed CSS is needed (for the fastest possible page load) but odd comments are still needed within the compressed CSS. Enter the **loud comment**.

A loud comment will be retained in the output CSS, even if the compressed option is chosen. Here's an example of how to create a loud comment:

```
/*! I am loud; hear me roar */
#main {
  color: #999;
  .content {
    color: #bfbfbf;
  }
}
```

It follows the same conventions as a normal CSS comment but the first character of the comment is an exclamation mark. With the compressed output style set, the output CSS would be this:

```
/* I am loud; hear me roar */#main{color:#999}#main
.content{color:#bfbfbf}
```

Even though the resultant CSS is squished together in the smallest amount of space possible, the loud comment is still present. This is really handy because if there are certain comments that need to be retained (copyright notices being an oft-cited example) in the code, if they are included with a loud comment, they always make it through to the production CSS.

Enable relative assets

The final part of the `config.rb` file we will concern ourselves with is the setting for relative paths. By default, the `config.rb` file includes this section:

```
# To enable relative paths to assets via compass helper functions.
Uncomment:
# relative_assets = true
```

This setting (not enabled by default so just uncomment it) allows Compass helpers to know that if an image is specified (for example), it knows where to find it relative to the CSS (as the paths for each have already been defined).

For example, typically when writing CSS there may be a path to an image used for a background as follows:

```
background-image: url('../img/image.jpg');
```

I'm sure you've suffered like me; get the path wrong and no image shows up in the design. Compass eliminates this issue with a simple helper. Instead, in the Sass file we can write the following code:

```
background-image: image-url('image.jpg');
```

Notice the `image-url` part instead of the usual `url`? This is a little Compass helper that equates to the path specified for images in the `config.rb` file. Using this, if all a project's images were moved, it's only necessary to update the image path in the `config.rb` file, regenerate the CSS file, and all the paths will match the new setting in the output CSS. Beautiful!

Now we've covered the essential functionality of the `config.rb` file, let's consider how to structure our code using **partial** files.

Creating and using partial files

Those who have written CSS for some time will remember it was once popular to split large CSS files into separate files for maintainability. For example, there might be a file for the header styles called `header.css`, another for the sidebar called `sidebar.css`, and one for the footer called `footer.css`. These would be imported into the main style sheet using import rules as follows:

```
@import url("header.css");
@import url("footer.css");
@import url("sidebar.css");
```

However, when building websites, it's now fairly widely accepted that the frontend code (the HTML, JavaScript, and CSS that is sent to the end-user) is delivered faster when there are fewer HTTP requests. Each file used on a page, whether HTML, JavaScript, CSS, image, or font makes up a separate HTTP request. As such, although it's possible to import additional CSS files using the `@import` rule, it's bad practice.

HTTP2 and SPDY

In the future, it is likely it won't be as necessary to sweat over the number of HTTP requests a site generates. Most browsers these days are limited to 6 connections at once. However, HTTP2 and Google's SPDY specifications will ease that limitation. The following link shows some slides by Andreas Bjärlestam that give a good overview:

`http://www.slideshare.net/bjarlestam/spdy-11723049`

In recent times, conscientious developers have concatenated any separate CSS files before upload (or used a system on the server to perform the concatenation and compression automatically). However, that often introduces another job and something else to remember when moving from development to production. Why do something a system can do for you?

Sass provides maintainability and production ready code

Sass offers the best of both worlds with partial files. As the name suggests, partial files aren't intended to be used in their own right. Rather, the intention is to use them as modular component parts of another, primary style sheet(s). Therefore, in the situation described previously, using Sass, a number of partial files such as `_header.scss` and `_footer.scss` would be created and then imported into the main file. For example:

```
@import "partials/header";
@import "partials/sidebar";
```

On compile, Sass will import the partials and output the relevant CSS where they are placed. Therefore, things such as `reset` or `normalize` partials are typically placed near the top of the main Sass file, while things such as `print` styles would typically be placed at the bottom. Let's take a look at how partial files work in practice.

We'll create a partial file for our `normalize` styles and then use the `@import` directive to bring those files in near the beginning of our main Sass file (which we're calling `styles.scss`).

Reset or Normalize?

There's no right or wrong when it comes to `reset` or `normalize` styles. If unfamiliar with either of these, they are included as the first set of rules within a style sheet. They either reset or normalize inconsistencies in the way that different browsers render elements by default.

Normalize (`http://necolas.github.com/normalize.css/`) takes a more subtle approach than a reset, 'normalizing' differences between browsers rather than resetting them completely. I tend to use Normalize and adjust the settings it provides according to the needs of the project.

Within the Sass folder of the project, create a folder called `partials`. Now within that, create a file called `_normalize.scss`. Notice the underscore before the file name? That's important. Without that, (for example, if it was just called `normalize.scss`), Sass and Compass will assume the file needs compiling when saved and will produce a separate file called `normalize.css`, which is not what we want.

So now we have a blank `_normalize.scss` file in our partials folder. Let's go and grab the Normalize styles. We can get the standard CSS version at `http://necolas.github.com/normalize.css/` and paste that in (remember valid CSS is also valid SCSS). Alternatively, grab one of the many Sass versions of Normalize that are available. I used the Sass version at `https://github.com/kristerkari/normalize.scss`

(my own fork of that repository is at `https://github.com/benfrain/normalize.scss` in case the original goes anywhere).

The Sass version has a few niceties such as being able to easily remove support for older versions of Internet Explorer, but don't sweat it for now, either the SCSS or CSS version is fine for our needs; just get the contents pasted into the `partials/_normalize.scss` file and save it. Well done, your first partial file is made. Now let's use it.

Importing a partial file

In the root of the Sass folder, create a blank file called `styles.scss`. Now add the following lines to the top:

```
@import "compass";
@import "partials/normalize";
```

Here we are doing two things; firstly we are importing Compass into our Sass file so that we can use all the great Compass features we will be looking at throughout this book. Next we are importing the `_normalize.scss` file we just made. Notice that we don't need to specify the file extension; Sass is smart enough to know what to do.

I'm assuming you have your system set to compile Sass on save. If not, you'll need to do that. Remember, it's done by either running `compass watch` from the command line or adding the project to the GUI program you've chosen to use (CodeKit, LiveReload, Scout, and the like).

Now save the Sass file and open the resultant CSS file. The normalize CSS declarations should be generated in the output format specified in the `config.rb` file (for example, `nested` or `compressed`).

See, partials are as easy as that. Just create a file for any chunk of CSS that needs to be sectioned off and import it where needed. There are no right or wrong ways to modularize files and styles in this manner. We'll do things a certain way in this book, but that doesn't mean you have to. Just define a method that works best for the way you or your team works.

If you were paying attention through *Chapter 1, Getting Started with Sass and Compass*, (and if you weren't, shame on you), you'll know that Sass can make use of variables for values. Variables can be defined anywhere in a Sass file, but as we're getting the hang of these partial things, to keep things nice and tidy, we'll create a new partial for all our variables and then import that variable file into our main `styles.scss` file. Here goes:

Create a new blank file in the partials folder called `_variables.scss`. In the main `styles.scss` file (in the root of the `sass` folder), amend the first lines to read as follows:

```
@import "compass";
@import "partials/variables";
@import "partials/normalize";
```

Here, after importing Compass, we are importing the _variables.scss partial and then the _normalize.scss partial. We'll be making and importing lots of partial files in the forthcoming chapters, but the convention is the same; make a partial file, add some code, and then import the partial where it's needed.

Notice that the variables partial file is imported before the normalize partial file? This is because by bringing all the variables in first, they are then able to be used in any Sass files listed afterwards. This is important. If attempting to use a variable before it is defined, Sass will produce an 'Undefined variable' error.

The moral of the story is this: define variables before writing or importing anything that uses them. If you don't want a separate file for your variables, ensure they are defined before they are referenced.

The syntax for writing variables in Sass

At present, the partial _variables.scss file we just made is empty. Let's fix that. The syntax for defining a variable in Sass is the dollar sign, followed by the variable name, a colon, and then the value to be assigned to the variable. For example:

```
$variable-name: value;
```

A typical use for variables is to define color values. That way, a simple, easy to remember name can be used for colors used throughout a project. We're going to do that here.

Now, there are many amazing things that Sass can do to manipulate color, and that's covered in depth in *Chapter 4, Manipulate Color with Ease*. For now we'll just make some variable names and assign hex color values to them. In the variables file, add the following values:

```
$color1: #FF0000; // Red
$color2: #FFBF00; // Orange
$color3: #FFFF00; // Yellow
$color4: #7FFF00; // Green
$color5: #007FFF; // Light Blue
$color6: #00FFFF; // Cyan
$color7: #0000FF; // Blue
$color8: #7F00FF; // Purple
$color9: #FF00FF; // Magenta
$color10: #000; // Black
$color11: #fff; // White
```

Naming variables is never easy. While I have given colors arbitrary names here (so that the values can be changed and the variable won't lose meaning), it would be equally sensible to name the variables more semantically (for example, $red for red and $light-blue for light blue). This would make them easier to remember but they would suffer the risk of making no sense if the value for red changed to a blue color for example. There's no one correct way to name the variables. Just use whatever works for you.

Excellent! We have now created a number of variables we can use elsewhere in the project. Before we get into that in future chapters, it's time for a brief but important diversion; to understand the different ways we can comment our code in Sass.

Sass comment formats

There are two different ways to add comments into Sass files.

Standard CSS comments

As any standard CSS file is also a valid Sass (.scss) file, it stands to reason we can comment as we would in standard CSS:

```
/* Here is a normal CSS comment */
```

Remember, using this format alongside the compressed output option will mean that the comment is removed from the resultant CSS. However, if not using the compressed option, the comment will be retained in the CSS.

Sass single line comments

Sass also allows the use of a double forward slash to define the beginning of a single line comment. This is the same manner in which JavaScript files can be commented; anything written after the double forward slash on the same line becomes a comment. Here's an example from the variable file we just made:

```
$color9: #FF00FF; // Magenta
```

Here the comment has been added after a variable has been defined. However it could also be used at the beginning of a line. For example:

```
// Here is a Sass only comment
```

No Sass comments written in this manner are output to the CSS file. Therefore, this can be useful for comments that should be retained in the Sass files (for legibility or aiding team members who may need to read and use the Sass files).

Perhaps use the Sass comment style to divide major sections of styles as follows:

```
// ======================================
// Here is a main section divide
// ======================================
```

And then subsections as follows:

```
// Here is a sub section divide
// ======================================
```

However, it's up to you how you want to comment your Sass files!

Don't forget, we've also learned how to write 'loud' comments when we need them. As mentioned, loud comments are perfect for copyright notices and the like. To write a loud comment, use the syntax for a standard CSS comment, but ensure that an exclamation mark is the first character used:

```
/*! Remember me, I'm loud! */
```

A basic index.html file

As Sass produces standard CSS files, nothing in the markup of your web pages need change. So, for example, in the blank `index.html` file we created in the root of our project, you can use a standard document structure, similar to the following example:

```
<!doctype html>
<!--[if lt IE 7]> <html class="no-js lt-ie9 lt-ie8 lt-ie7" lang="en">
<![endif]-->
<!--[if IE 7]> <html class="no-js lt-ie9 lt-ie8" lang="en">
<![endif]-->
<!--[if IE 8]> <html class="no-js lt-ie9" lang="en"> <![endif]-->
<!--[if gt IE 8]><!--> <html class="no-js" lang="en"> <!--<![endif]-->
<head>
  <meta charset="utf-8">
  <title></title>
  <meta name="description" content="">
  <meta name="viewport" content="width=device-width">
  <link rel="stylesheet" href="css/styles.css">
```

```
</head>
<body>
  <header>

  </header>
  <div role="main">

  </div>
  <footer>

  </footer>

  <script src="js/plugins.js"></script>
  <script src="js/main.js"></script>

</body>
</html>
```

The only point to note is that the CSS file being linked to matches the file and path being produced with the Sass file.

A base for future projects

At this point, we have a good skeletal structure for any project:

- A basic folder and file structure for typical website assets
- A Compass `config.rb` file set up
- The various paths for images and the like set

This base project should be generic enough that it can be used as a starting point for almost any future web project. Therefore, if everything is looking good, make a copy of the folder housing this project and rename the copied folder to 'base' (or whatever you like). This can then be used as a starting point for future Compass-based Sass projects without needing to run any commands. Instead, you'll be able to copy it, amend it to suit, and get coding.

Summary

In this chapter, we have learned how important it is to understand partial files for easy compartmentalization of code. We now also understand the various ways we can comment code, enabling us to write more legible and maintainable Sass files that are easier for us and others to work with.

We also now understand the mechanics of the `config.rb` file—how we can use it to alter output styles, output comments to aid debugging, and alter the paths for the output CSS.

I think we have covered all the essential groundwork now. Hopefully you are feeling like Daniel-san from Karate Kid*—the essentials have bedded in and it's now time to start with the good stuff.

In the next chapter, we are going to learn and master the workhorse tools of writing Sass. nesting, placeholders, @extend, and mixins. The *"wow"* stuff starts here.

*If you have not seen Karate Kid, don't worry. It's not essential to understanding Sass and Compass. Besides, it could lead to you spending too long standing on one foot with your hands raised in a peculiar position.

3
Nesting, Extend, Placeholders, and Mixins

In *Chapter 2, Setting up a Sass and Compass project*, we learnt some core principles of setting up a project with Sass and Compass. For example, the various ways in which Sass allows code to be commented, how partial files can be used to more easily compartmentalize sections of code, and crucially, how to alter the output style of the generated CSS.

In this chapter, we will look at the capabilities of Sass and Compass when it comes to actually writing styles. These are the core capabilities likely to be employed when working with Sass and Compass day-to-day.

In this chapter, we will learn:

- What nesting is and how it allows styles to be modularized
- How the `@extend` directive allows us to extend existing rules
- To use placeholder selectors to extend styles only when needed
- What mixins are and how we can use them to easily produce oft-needed code
- How to write a mixin for our own purposes

Styling a site with Sass and Compass

Personally, while abstract examples are fine, I find it difficult to fully understand concepts until I put them into practice. With that in mind, at this point I'm going to amend the markup in our project's `index.html` file, so we have some markup to flex our growing Sass and Compass muscles on.

We're going to build up a basic home page for this book. Through this and the later chapters we can use the Sass and Compass techniques we're learning to style the markup. Hopefully, while the contents of the page may not be entirely relevant to your next project (unless of course you're writing a book on Sass and Compass, in which case you're in luck), the basic layout and structure will be common enough to be of help. If you want to see how things turn out, you can point your browser at `http://sassandcompass.com`, as that's what we'll be building.

The markup for the home page is fairly simple. It consists of a header with links, navigation made up of list items, images, and content and a footer area. Pasting the home page markup here will span a few pages (and be extremely dull to read). Therefore, if you would like to see the markup at this point, refer to the relevant chapter code. Don't get too hung up on the specifics of the markup. It's probable it will change from chapter to chapter.

Let me be clear. The actual code, selectors used, and the finished webpage that we'll create are not important. The Sass and Compass techniques and tools we use to create them are.

> You can download the code from the book's page at `http://packtpub.com` and also from `http://sassandcompass.com`

At this point, here's how the page looks in the browser:

Wow, what a looker! Thankfully, with Sass and Compass we're going to knock this into shape in no time at all.

> Notice that in the source code there are semantically named classes in the markup. Some people dislike this practice, but I have found that it makes it easier to create more modular and maintainable code.
>
> A full discussion on the reasoning behind using classes against styling elements themselves is a little beyond the scope of this book. However, a good book on this topic is *SMACSS* by Jonathan Snook (`http://smacss.com`). It's not essential to adhere slavishly to the conventions he describes, but it's a great start in thinking about how to structure and write style sheets in general.

First, let's open the `_normalize.scss` partial file and amend the default styles for links (changing the default text-underline to a dotted bottom border) and remove the padding and margin for the `ul` tags.

Now I think about this, before we get knee-deep in code, a little more organization is called for.

Separating the layout from visuals

Before getting into nesting, `@extend`, `placeholders`, and mixins, it makes sense to create some partial files for organizing the styles.

Rather than create a partial Sass file for each structural area (the header, footer, and navigation), and lump all the visual styles relevant inside, we can structure the code in a slightly more abstract manner.

> There is no right or wrong way to split up Sass files. However, it's worth looking at mature and respected projects such as Twitter Bootstrap (`https://github.com/twitter/bootstrap`) and Foundation from Zurb (`https://github.com/zurb/foundation`) to see how they organize their code.

We'll create a partial file called `_base.scss` that will contain some base styles:

```scss
body {
    font-size: 1em;
    line-height: 1.4;
}
::-moz-selection {
    background: $color1;
    text-shadow: none;
}
::selection {
    background: $color1;
    text-shadow: none;
}
```

Then a partial file called `_layout.scss`. That will only contain rules pertaining to visual layout and positioning of the main page areas (the previously mentioned header, footer, aside, section, and navigation). Here are the initial styles being added into the `_layout.scss` partial file:

```scss
* {
    -webkit-box-sizing: border-box;
    -moz-box-sizing: border-box;
    box-sizing: border-box;
}
body {
  max-width: 1200px;
    margin: auto;
}
header[role="banner"],footer[role="contentinfo"] {
  width: 100%;
  display: block;
}
nav[role="navigation"] {
  width: 25%;
  float: left;
}
.main-content {
  width: 70%;
  float: right;
}
footer[role="contentinfo"] {
  clear: both;
}
```

There is nothing particular to Sass there, it's all standard CSS.

Debug help in the browser

Thanks to the popularity of Sass there are now experimental features in browsers to make debugging Sass even easier. When inspecting an element with developer tools, the source file and line number is provided, making it easier to find the offending selector. For Chrome, here's a step-by-step explanation: `http://benfra.in/1z1`

Alternatively, if using Firefox, check out the FireSass extension: `https://addons.mozilla.org/en-us/firefox/addon/firesass-for-firebug/`

Let's create another partial file called `_modules.scss`. This will contain all the modular pieces of code. This means, should we need to move the `.testimonial` section (which should be a modular section) in the source code, it's not necessary to move it from one partial file to another (which would be the case if the partial files were named according to their existing layout).

The `_module.scss` file will probably end up being the largest file in the Sass project, as it will contain all the aesthetics for the items on the page. However, the hope is that these modular pieces of code will be flexible enough to look good, regardless of the structural constraints defined in the `_layout.scss` partial file.

If working on a very large project, it may be worth splitting the modules into sub-folders. Just create a sub-folder and import the file. For example, if there was a partial called `_callouts.scss` in a sub-folder called `modules`, it could be imported using the following code:

```
@import "partials/modules/callouts";
```

Here is the contents of the amended `styles.scss` file:

```
@import "compass";
@import "partials/variables";
@import "partials/normalize";
@import "partials/base";
@import "partials/layout";
@import "partials/modules";
```

A quick look at the HTML in the browser shows the basic layout styles applied:

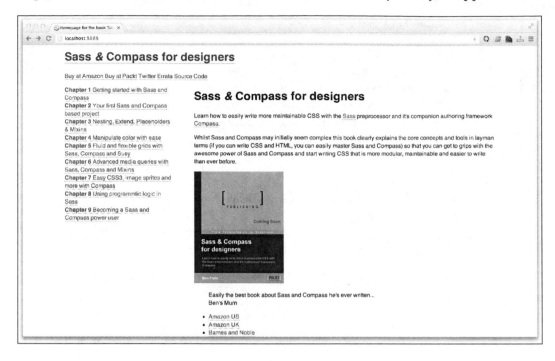

With that done, let's look at how Sass's ability to nest styles can help us make modules of code.

What nesting is and how it facilitates modules of code

In *Chapter 1, Getting started with Sass and Compass*, we looked briefly at nesting. It provides the ability to nest styles within one another. This provides a handy way to write mini blocks of modular code.

Nesting syntax

With a normal CSS style declaration, there is a selector, then an opening curly brace, and then any number of property and value pairs, followed by a closing curly brace. For example:

```
.css {
  display: block;
}
```

Where Sass differs is that before the closing curly brace, you can nest another rule within. What do I mean by that? Consider this example:

```
a {
  color: $color7;
  &:hover,&:focus {
    color: $color5;
  }
  &:visited,&:active {
    color: $color4;
  }
}
```

In the previous code, a color has been set for the link tag using a variable. Then the `hover` and `focus` state have been nested within the main anchor style with a different color set. Furthermore, styles for the visited and active state have been nested with an alternate color defined.

> Remember in *Chapter 2*, *Setting Up a Sass and Compass project*, we made a partial file called `_variables.scss` and assigned a number of hex color values to the variables. That's what we are referencing in the previous code. To reference a variable, simply write the dollar sign ($) and then the name of the variable, for example, `$variable`.

When compiled, this produces the following CSS:

```
a {

  color: blue;

}

a:hover, a:focus {

  color: #007fff;

}

a:visited, a:active {

  color: chartreuse;

}
```

> Notice that Sass is also smart enough to know that the hex value `#7FFF00` is actually the color called chartreuse, and when it has generated the CSS it has converted it to the CSS color name.

How can this be used practically? Let's look at the markup for the list of navigation links on the home page. Each currently looks like this:

```html
<nav role="navigation">
    <ul class="chapter-list">
        <li class="chapter-summary">
            <a href="chapter1.html">
                <b>Chapter 1</b>
                <span>Getting started with Sass and Compass</span>
            </a>
        </li>
```

I've omitted the additional list items and closing tags in the previous code for the sake of brevity. From a structure point of view, each list item contains an anchor link with a `<b>` tag and a `<span>` tag within. Here's the initial Sass nested styles that have been added into the `_modules.scss` partial to control that section:

```scss
.chapter-summary {
  a {
    display: block;
    padding: .5em;
    color: $color10;
    opacity: .7;
    border: none;
    &:hover {
      opacity: 1;
    }
    &:visited {
      opacity: .9;
    }
    b {
      display: block;
    }
    span {
      display: block;
      font-size: .8em;
    }
  }
}
```

Notice that the rules are being nested inside the class .chapter-summary. That's because it then limits the scope of the nested styles to only apply to elements within a list item with a class of .chapter-summary. However, remember that if the styles can be re-used elsewhere, it isn't necessarily the best practice to nest them, as they may become too specific.

The nesting of the selectors in this manner partially mirrors the structure of the HTML, so it's easy to see that the styles nested within only apply to those that are similarly structured in the markup.

We're starting with the outermost element that needs to be styled (the `<li class="chapter-summary">`) and then nesting the first element within that. In this instance, it's the anchor tag. Then further styles have been nested for the hover and visited states along with the `<b>` and `<span>` tags.

I tend to add focus and active states at the end of a project, but that's a personal thing. If you're likely to forget them, by all means add them at the same time you add hover.

Here's the generated CSS from that block:

```css
.chapter-summary a {
  display: block;
  padding: .5em;
  color: black;
  opacity: .7;
  border: none;
}
.chapter-summary a:hover {
  opacity: 1;
}
.chapter-summary a:visited {
  opacity: .9;
}
.chapter-summary a b {
  display: block;
}
.chapter-summary a span {
  display: block;
  font-size: .8em;
}
```

The nested styles are generated with a degree of specificity that limits their scope; they will only apply to elements within a `<li class="chapter-summary">`.

It's possible to nest all manner of styles within one another. Classes, IDs, pseudo classes; Sass doesn't much care. For example, let's suppose the `<li>` elements need to have a dotted border, except for the last one. Let's take advantage of the last-child CSS pseudo class in combination with nesting and add this section:

```
.chapter-summary {
  border-bottom: 2px dotted;
  &:last-child {
    border: none;
  }
}
/* other styles */
```

That will generate the following CSS:

```
.chapter-summary {
  border-bottom: 2px dotted;
}
.chapter-summary:last-child {
  border: none;
}
```

The parent selector

Notice that any pseudo selector that needs to be nested in Sass is prefixed with the ampersand symbol (&), then a colon (:). The ampersand symbol has a special meaning when nesting. It always references the parent selector. It's perfect for defining pseudo classes as it effectively says 'the parent plus this pseudo element'. However, there are other ways it can work too, for example, nesting a few related selectors and expressing different relationships between them:

```
.main {
  .content {
    width: 70%;
  }
  .content & {
    width: 100%;
  }
  .content & {
    .two & {
      color: pink;
    }
  }
}
```

This actually results in the following CSS:

```
.main .content {
  width: 70%;
}
.content .main {
  width: 100%;
}
.two .content .main {
  color: pink;
}
```

We have effectively reversed the selectors while nesting by using the & parent selector.

Chaining selectors

It's also possible to create chained selectors using the parent selector. Consider this:

```
.selector-one {
  &.selector-two {
    color: green;
  }
}
```

That will compile to this:

```
.selector-one.selector-two {
  color: green;
}
```

That will only select an element that has both HTML classes, namely selector-one and selector-two.

The parent selector is perfect for pseudo selectors and at odd times its necessary to chain selectors, but beyond that I couldn't find much practical use for it, until I saw this set of slides by Sass guru Brandon Mathis http://speakerdeck.com/u/imathis/p/sass-compass-the-future-of-stylesheets-now. In this, he illustrates how to use the parent selector for nesting a Modernizr relevant rule.

Easy Modernizr styles with the parent selector

Modernizr provides the perfect situation in which to utilize the parent selector. When a fork is needed in CSS, Modernizr can save the day. If forking code sounds alien, fear not, this will make more sense shortly. This is a bit of a tangent but I think it's worthwhile.

Let's download Modernizr (`http://modernizr.com`) and save it into the `js` folder. Then add a reference to it in the `<head>` section of the web page:

```
<script src="js/modernizr.2.6.2.min.js"></script>
```

> If you have no idea what Modernizr is or how to use it, I'd recommend starting with this blog post: `http://benfra.in/1y2`.

Let's use the font called **Sansation** by Bernt Montag as the main body text font for the site. There's an **@font-face** version of the font available free from Font Squirrel (`http://www.fontsquirrel.com/fonts/Sansation`):

The font files have been copied into a folder called `fonts` inside the `css` folder. Here's the hierarchy of the `css` folder in the OS X Finder:

Make a partial file for fonts

We'll create another partial file called `_fonts.scss`. Inside that file will be references to any web fonts needed. Before that, let's import the partial file into the main `styles.scss` file:

```
@import "compass";
@import "partials/variables";
@import "partials/fonts";
@import "partials/normalize";
@import "partials/base";
@import "partials/layout";
@import "partials/modules";
```

Now, we need to set up the font files in the `_fonts.scss` partial file. To help matters, the downloaded Font Squirrel font includes a CSS file (`stylesheet.css`) with the relevant font files referenced. However, it needs amending before pasting it into the `_fonts.scss` partial file.

First we're going to keep each font used in a sub-folder, just to keep things tidy. Furthermore, we'll use a Compass URL helper to reference the fonts. So instead of:

```
src: url
```

In the downloaded code, we will write:

```
src: font-url
```

The Compass `font-url` helper is worth using as it allows us to save the font files in the `fonts` sub-folder of the `css` folder. Then, because we added a `fonts_dir` directory in the `config.rb` file, Sass and Compass know that they need to look for the fonts in that location.

Changing the font with Modernizr and the parent selector

Now, with that web font set up it's time to finally use that parent selector to fork the CSS styles with the help of Modernizr. In the `_body.scss` partial file, the first rule looks like this:

```
body {

    font-size: 1em;

    line-height: 1.4;

    font-family: "SansationRegular","HelveticaNeue-Light","Helvetica
Neue", Helvetica, Arial, sans-serif;

    // Modernizr fallback for when there is no fontface support

    .no-fontface & {

        font-size: 1.05em;

    }

}
```

The `font-family` property has been added with the value of "`SansationRegular`" first, then a number of secondary fonts (using a standard font stack).

Sansation looks fine at `1em` size, but if the browser needs to use one of the backup fonts (if the device doesn't support `@font-face`), the other fonts in the stack look a little too big. In this eventuality, it would be good if the font size could be slightly less. Modernizr can help us create this fork.

When @font-face support is missing, Modernizr adds a class of .no-font-face to the HTML. In that instance, the nested rule gets applied (thanks to it being more specific and later in the cascade) amending the font-size slightly. Our nested rule actually produces the following CSS:

```
body {

  font-size: 1em;

  line-height: 1.4;

  font-family: "SansationRegular", "HelveticaNeue-Light", "Helvetica
Neue", Helvetica, Arial, sans-serif;

}

.no-fontface body {

  font-size: 1.05em;

}
```

Lovely! By using this nesting method along with the parent selector, all these related styles are grouped together in the Sass files. Also, thanks to Modernizr, browsers that support @font-face and those that don't get a relevant font-size.

 Remember that the parent selector isn't needed for nesting inline elements (<span>, <i>, <b> and likewise), classes, or IDs. Just nest them normally.

Dangers of excessive nesting

It's possible to nest styles many levels deep. Here's an example of nesting using IDs, classes, and pseudo selectors:

```
.nesting {
  .class {
    width: 100%;
  }
  #id {
    width: 100%;
  }
  &:hover {
    color: $color7;
  }
  .multi-nesting {
    .class-within {
      width: 90%;
```

```
        #id_within {
          width: 90%;
          &:hover {
            color: $color4;
          }
        }
      }
    }
  }
}
```

However, when I see chunks of code like that, I start to get a little concerned. There is a real danger that nesting this many levels deep will create CSS rules that are too specific. For example, here is the generated CSS from that little block:

```
.nesting .class {
  width: 100%;
}
.nesting #id {
  width: 100%;
}
.nesting:hover {
  color: blue;
}
.nesting .multi-nesting .class-within {
  width: 90%;
}
.nesting .multi-nesting .class-within #id_within {
  width: 90%;
}
.nesting .multi-nesting .class-within #id_within:hover {
  color: chartreuse;
}
```

As you can see, the further into the nesting we get, the more specific the outputted CSS selector becomes. In the final rule there, we are selecting a hover state on an ID selector that will only be relevant if it's within a class of class-within, that is also a child of a class multi-nesting that is also a child of a class nesting. To cut a long story short, you should probably just use the following (not nested within anything else):

```
#id_within {
  width: 90%;
  &:hover {
    color: $color4;
  }
}
```

That would output the following CSS:

```
#id_within {
  width: 90%;
}
#id_within:hover {
  color: chartreuse;
}
```

This means that the element with an ID of `id_within` can be moved anywhere else in the markup and still get the styles applied. Here's a simple rule I try and abide by: only make rules as specific as they need to be, and if nesting, try not to go more than three levels deep.

Are ID selectors bad?

There's a growing sentiment in the web developer community that if possible, when choosing selectors in CSS, IDs are a bad choice. As ever in web development, I think it depends.

The genesis of the thinking stems from the fact that ID selectors are limited by nature (a page is invalid if a single ID exists more than once on any page) and therefore, it makes rules bound to ID selectors limiting (as any styles can't be re-used elsewhere). In addition, ID selectors are more specific than a class style, and that makes it difficult to override those declarations later on.

Those are valid concerns. However, there may be times where the same ID appears on every page and you are confident you won't need to override it. In that case, don't get hung up on using an ID as a styling hook. If the option for using a class name exists, take it, but don't worry about using an ID if necessary. For a little more info on the subject, you might want to take a look at the following blog post: http://benfra.in/1yq

It's also worth knowing that as long as support for IE6 isn't necessary, it's possible to use an attribute selector to style an ID that will hook the style without the massive specificity that ordinarily comes from using an ID selector. For example:

```
[id="id-name"] {}
```

Instead of using:

```
#id-name {}
```

Nesting namespaces

Sass also lets you nest namespaced CSS properties. That's any CSS property that has a namespace reserved. For example, border has border-left, border-right, border-top, and border-bottom. Font has font-weight, font-family, and font-size. Here's an example of nesting the namespaced border property:

```
.nesting-namespace-properties {
  border: {
    top: 1px dashed $color7;
    right: 1px dotted $color5;
    bottom: 2px solid $color8;
    left: 1px solid $color4;
  }
}
```

That would compile to the following CSS:

```
.nesting-namespace-properties {
  border-top: 1px dashed blue;
  border-right: 1px dotted #007fff;
  border-bottom: 2px solid #7f00ff;
  border-left: 1px solid chartreuse;
}
```

With Sass, it's possible to define the namespaced part of the property and then nest the possible variants within it. The same thing could be done with the margin and padding property (where there are variants such as margin-left and margin right). Personally, I find it easier to rely on the standard CSS shorthand syntax in those instances.

For the sake of clarity, using the standard CSS shorthand syntax for a margin, to remove the margin on all sides of an element except the bottom, write:

```
.margin {
  margin: 0 0 1em 0;
}
```

> When writing this CSS shorthand (which is applicable to the padding property too) remember that the values defined left to right in the code, relate clockwise starting at the top (for example, first top, then right, then bottom, and finally left). Also, be aware that when a value is zero, there is no need to declare a unit of measure (such as em or px).

When writing Sass, nesting namespaced properties isn't something I do very often. I prefer the clarity of having the full property listed. However, it's a preference thing, so be aware that nesting can be used in this manner.

While we have acknowledged that nesting should be used considerately, it is incredibly handy for defining modular sections of code. For example, here are some basic nested styles to make a module for the `<aside class="testimonial">` area:

```scss
.testimonial {
  background-color: #eee;
  border-top: 2px solid #ddd;
  border-bottom: 2px solid #ddd;
  padding: 1em 2em;
  > img {
    display: inline-block;
    width: 17%;
  }
  blockquote {
    margin: 0 0 0 3%;
    padding: 0 .5em;
    width: 76%;
    font-family: $blockquote;
    font-size: 2.4em;
    font-style:italic;
    display: inline-block;
    vertical-align: top;
    footer {
      font-size: .6em;
      border-top: 2px dotted #ddd;
      margin: 20px 0 0 0;
      padding: 10px 0 0 0;
    }
  }
  blockquote.small {
    font-size: .9em;
  }
}
```

Notice here that at the bottom of the module we have added a style for the `<blockquote>` tag if it also has a class of `small` added. This is so that if the testimonial needed to be moved into an area with constricted space such as a sidebar (this is a different situation than a smaller viewport, we'll get onto that in *Chapter 6, Advanced Media Queries with Sass and Mixins*) the font size isn't too big. For example:

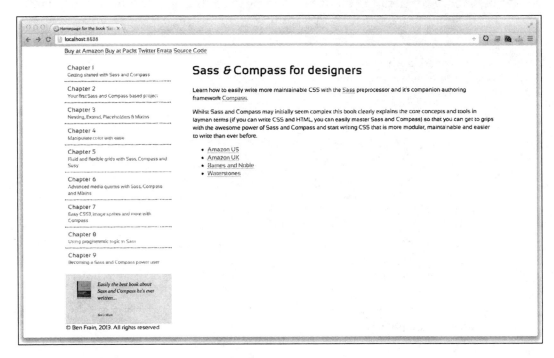

 It may be preferable to add an entirely different class to cater for these different visual permutations. So instead of a `.blockquote.small` class (that will get applied when both blockquote and small HTML classes are present on the HTML element), we might use `.blockquote--small` and add that HTML class to the element to denote the small variant of the original block instead.

We've also defined colors as hex values here. When using Sass and Compass there is little reason to do that, and we'll switch those out for variables and color functions in *Chapter 4, Manipulate Color with Ease.*

Finally, notice how a variable has been used for the font-family of the `blockquote`. The variable itself is just a font-stack. Here's that variable in the `_variables.scss` partial file:

```
$blockquote: Constantia, "Lucida Bright", Lucidabright,
"Lucida Serif", Lucida, "DejaVu Serif", "Bitstream Vera Serif",
"Liberation Serif", Georgia, serif;
```

With those styles added, this is how our testimonial area renders:

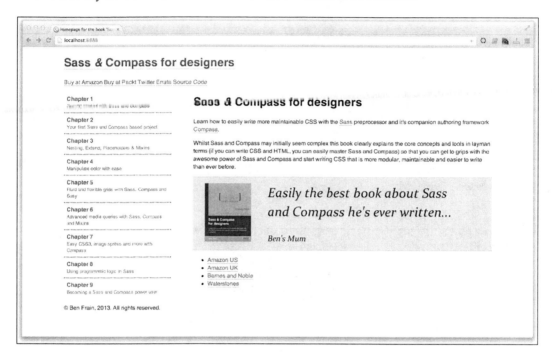

Using the @extend directive to extend existing rules

The `@extend` directive is used to extend another style. It allows any style to inherit the properties and values defined in another. Suppose there are a few elements to style that share some characteristics; they are a prime candidate for the `@extend` directive. Let's try an abstract example. We need to create a few boxes. A standard box, a success box, an information box, and finally a warning box. Consider this code:

```scss
// Box
.box {
  padding: 2em;
  color: $color10;
  background-color: $color11;
}
// Warning Box
.warning-box {
  @extend .box;
  border: 2px dotted $color1;
}
// Success Box
.success-box {
  @extend .box;
  border: 2px dotted $color4;
}
// Information Box
.info-box {
  @extend .box;
  border: 2px dotted $color7;
}
```

First there is a style for the basic box, then each variation extends the box but has it's own different color border. This is the CSS code it generates:

```css
.box, .warning-box, .success-box, .info-box {
  padding: 2em;
  color: black;
  background-color: white;
}

.warning-box {
  border: 2px dotted red;
}

.success-box {
  border: 2px dotted chartreuse;
}

.info-box {
  border: 2px dotted blue;
}
```

Sass is smart enough to group the shared styles under a single combined selector. Using the @extend directive in this manner prevents endless repetition of code for similar elements.

Now, notice in this example, our first rule for .box class wouldn't actually be used. It's being declared for the sole purpose of extending. That may seem a little wasteful and, thankfully, the smart people working on Sass have already got a solution. In situations where we want to define rules purely to extend them elsewhere, we can use placeholder selectors. Let's look at how they work.

Using placeholder selectors to extend styles only when needed

We've just looked at how the @extend directive can extend an existing rule. However, in situations when a rule is being created purely to extend it, use a placeholder selector instead. Here's our prior example written with a placeholder selector on the first rule instead:

```
// Box
%box {
  padding: 2em;
  color: $color10;
  background-color: $color11;
}
// Warning Box
.warning-box {
  @extend %box;
  border: 2px dotted $color1;
}
// Success Box
.success-box {
  @extend %box;
  border: 2px dotted $color4;
}
// Information Box
.info-box {
  @extend %box;
  border: 2px dotted $color7;
}
```

Instead of the normal selector (a period for a class or hash/pound for an ID selector), use a percentage symbol (%) instead. Then use the `@extend` directive to extend it. Here is the code that compiles to:

```
.warning-box, .success-box, .info-box {
  padding: 2em;
  color: black;
  background-color: white;
}

.warning-box {
  border: 2px dotted red;
}

.success-box {
  border: 2px dotted chartreuse;
}

.info-box {
  border: 2px dotted blue;
}
```

By using the placeholder selector instead, it prevents surplus rules being generated unless they have been extended elsewhere. We'll use `placeholder` and `@extend` selectors frequently to build the styles for the homepage of `http://sassandcompass.com` as they are particularly handy when working with mixins.

What mixins are and how we can use them to easily produce oft-needed code

Nesting `@extend` and `placeholder` selectors are very convenient but they don't actually produce extra code. Mixins on the other hand do. Those readers who have been unfortunate enough to use Microsoft Word or Excel may have used macros. If so, think of mixins like macros.

Typically, a mixin is defined once, then included elsewhere in the Sass file and passed any optional arguments. Then, on compilation, it generates the relevant code.

That sounds pretty complicated and "programmer-ish". If such talk makes your palms go a little sweaty or your eyes glaze over, don't worry.

Compass has literally hundreds of ready-made mixins that address every conceivable CSS need. Don't want to dabble in writing mixins? Just use the ones that Compass provides; enjoy cross-browser compatibility that makes you feel heroic and thank the Compass team with a donation to the Compass's charityware cause: `http://umdf.org/compass`

However, for the curious, let's look at making a mixin and we'll soon get the hang of things.

Remember back when we added some content into our `_layout.scss` file, the first rule was this:

```
* {
  -webkit-box-sizing: border-box;
  -moz-box-sizing: border-box;
  box-sizing: border-box;
}
```

The star selector was used to select all elements and change the box-sizing model to `border-box`. To get the best browser support possible, the property was repeated a number of times with vendor prefixes (one for WebKit and another for Mozilla with the final official property and value pair listed last so that it supersedes the others, if present).

> In case you aren't aware of what the different box-sizing models do, the `border-box` model allows a width to be defined for an element and it takes into account borders, padding, and content. The size set is the size that gets painted to the screen. The alternative (and at this point more commonly used) `content-box` box-sizing model requires content, padding, and border to be factored-in when specifying the width/height of an element.
>
> Microsoft actually implemented `border-box` sizing way back in Internet Explorer 8, so browser support is good. As I'm not concerned about IE7 and below, I'm happy to use `border-box` here. To read more on the matter, head over to this excellent post by all-round web genius, Paul Irish, on the matter: `http://paulirish.com/2012/box-sizing-border-box-ftw/`

Let's write a little mixin here to generate this code for us. Let's create another partial file called `_mixins.scss` and import that into our main `styles.scss`. Here's what the import section looks like now:

```scss
@import "compass";
@import "partials/variables";
@import "partials/mixins";
@import "partials/fonts";
@import "partials/normalize";
@import "partials/base";
@import "partials/layout";
@import "partials/modules";
```

Notice, the mixins partial file has been imported after the variables partial, so any of the variables can be used in the mixins and then in turn any of the mixins can be used in the other files that come after. In the `_mixins.scss` partial file, we're adding this:

```scss
@mixin bs($bs-type) {
  -webkit-box-sizing: $bs-type;
  -moz-box-sizing: $bs-type;
  box-sizing: $bs-type;
}
```

Then, in the `_layout.scss` file, the first line is being amended to this:

```scss
* {
  @include bs(border-box);
}
```

When the Sass file is saved, the generated CSS looks as we hoped:

```css
* {
  -webkit-box-sizing: border-box;
  -moz-box-sizing: border-box;
  box-sizing: border-box;
}
```

So how did that actually happen? Let's go back and consider our mixin code and establish the basic syntax.

Basic mixin syntax

First of all, we declare the `@mixin` directive and name the mixin. In this instance, it's named `bs` (terser than using box-shadow), but it could have been called bananas (go ahead, I don't judge):

```scss
@mixin bs($bs-type) {
```

Then, immediately after the name, there is an opening parenthesis and what looks like a variable placed inside before a closing parenthesis.

The variable name here is acting as an argument. Think of arguments as optional parameters or settings that can be passed when including a mixin. In this instance, it will typically be either `content-box` or `border-box`.

After the opening curly brace is the code the mixin will actually generate, followed by the closing curly brace. Here's the complete mixin again:

```scss
@mixin bs($bs-type) {
  -webkit-box-sizing: $bs-type;
  -moz-box-sizing: $bs-type;
  box-sizing: $bs-type;
}
```

By placing the identical variable used as an argument at various places in the generated code, the mixin knows where to place the value.

I'm concerned that may sound more complex than it actually is, so let's do something silly to illustrate. Let's change the value of the argument being passed in the `_layout.scss` file to `one-that-works`:

```scss
* {
  @include bs(one-that-works);
}
```

Hopefully, you'll know what that is going to be generated in the CSS:

```scss
* {
  -webkit-box-sizing: one-that-works;
  -moz-box-sizing: one-that-works;
  box-sizing: one-that-works;
}
```

Whatever is passed as an argument to the mixin when it's included gets output into the generated code on compile.

> Sass will check for syntax errors on compile (missing semi-colons and the like) and display a suitable error indicating where the error is. While it can syntax check the code, it can't sanity check it. Sass doesn't know that `one-that-works` isn't a valid value for the box-sizing property so it will happily generate that for you in the CSS.

How to write mixins with defaults

Mixins can also be set with a default value. This means that you can include them without passing an argument and they will generate with a default value. Here's how:

```
@mixin bs($bs-type: border-box) {
   -webkit-box-sizing: $bs-type;
   -moz-box-sizing: $bs-type;
   box-sizing: $bs-type;
}
```

Can you see what changed? After the initial variable name, there is a colon, and then the value to be used as the default (border-box in this instance). Now, the mixin can be included like this:

```
* {
   @include bs;
}
```

And it will still generate this:

```
* {
   -webkit-box-sizing: border-box;
   -moz-box-sizing: border-box;
   box-sizing: border-box;
}
```

However, if needed, an argument can still be passed to it. For example:

```
* {
   @include bs(content-box);
}
```

And it would generate this:

```
* {
   -webkit-box-sizing: content-box;
   -moz-box-sizing: content-box;
   box-sizing: content-box;
}
```

If a mixin is needed that will be on lots of future projects, it might be preferable to set the mixin up so that it takes a global variable as the default value for an argument. That way, the default value will only be used if a value isn't specified in a global variable elsewhere.

This can be done by using the `!default` flag. Consider this example:

```scss
$defined-bs-type: border-box;
$defined-bs-type: sausages !default;
@mixin bs($bs-type: $defined-bs-type) {
  -webkit-box-sizing: $bs-type;
  -moz-box-sizing: $bs-type;
  box-sizing: $bs-type;
}
```

First, the variable `$defined-bs-type` has been assigned the value of `border-box`. On the next line, the same variable has been set a value of `sausages`, with the `!default` flag before the closing semi-colon. The rest of the mixin is as before. Then the mixin is being included in the `_layouts.scss` file like this:

```scss
* {
  @include bs;
}
```

Ordinarily, it might be expected that the value generated on compile would be `sausages`, as that is the last value assigned to the variable. However, the `!default` flag is telling Sass to only use this value if a different value hasn't been assigned elsewhere. Because a value has been assigned elsewhere (in the line above), it doesn't use the default. Instead, here's what is generated:

```scss
* {
  -webkit-box-sizing: border-box;
  -moz-box-sizing: border-box;
  box-sizing: border-box;
}
```

However, if the first value assignment of the variable is omitted:

```scss
$defined-bs-type: sausages !default;
@mixin bs($bs-type: $defined-bs-type) {
  -webkit-box-sizing: $bs-type;
  -moz-box-sizing: $bs-type;
  box-sizing: $bs-type;
}
```

This is the generated code:

```scss
* {
  -webkit-box-sizing: sausages;
  -moz-box-sizing: sausages;
  box-sizing: sausages;
}
```

Yet this still provides the flexibility to specifically pass an argument when including the mixin:

```
* {
  @include bs(content-box);
}
```

This passes the defined argument on compile to CSS:

```
* {
  -webkit-box-sizing: content-box;
  -moz-box-sizing: content-box;
  box-sizing: content-box;
}
```

The benefit of this approach is that when you have a few mixins built they can be carried from project to project. Then the value that needs assigning can be defined as a variable elsewhere (such as a `_variables.scss` partial file). Then, altering the value of that variable will affect every instance of the mixin.

Compass has heaps of great mixins of its own that can be used in this manner. There will be far more on the specifics of Compass in *Chapter 7, Easy CSS3, Image Sprites, and More with Compass.*

Compass, purveyor of the finest mixins

Want to see just how funky mixins can get? Head over to the Compass project page on GitHub: `https://github.com/chriseppstein/compass`. Many of the mixins in Compass often include additional geekery such as functions and variable arguments, and we'll take a look at some of that fun in later chapters.

For example, Compass has its own version of the box-sizing mixin itself, with some extra cleverness cooked in: `https://github.com/chriseppstein/compass/blob/stable/frameworks/compass/stylesheets/compass/css3/_box-sizing.scss`

Or look at the amount of work that has gone into making a beautiful cross-browser mixin for text-shadows (including the spread parameter where supported): `https://github.com/chriseppstein/compass/blob/stable/frameworks/compass/stylesheets/compass/css3/_text-shadow.scss`

A cautionary note about generated CSS

As noted in the first chapter, writing bad Sass will generate bad CSS. Overuse of nesting, @extend, and mixins can lead to bloated code and over-specific selectors. Therefore, apply the same level of common sense when writing Sass as you would when writing plain vanilla CSS (when I say vanilla CSS, I just mean normal CSS with no preprocessor involved in its creation). For example, only make rules as specific as they need to be, don't nest rules too deeply and don't repeat mixins unless necessary.

Getting the hang of writing Sass well from the outset is important. Using Sass and Compass to create CSS files means you will be less inclined to look at the final outputted CSS.

However, even if Sass and Compass don't generate CSS exactly as you would have written it by hand, remember that it is only the browser that actually consumes the compiled CSS (and at that point it should be compressed and illegible to humans anyway). Therefore as no human will actually need to read the generated CSS, it doesn't concern me one bit. As long as the CSS is as efficient for the browser as it can be and my Sass files make sense to others and myself, I'm happy.

CSS file size is a micro optimization

Take a look at the following URL at HTTP Archive. It shows the different types of file that make up a typical webpage: `http://httparchive.org/interesting.php#bytesperpage`. As you can see, CSS is the smallest content type. Therefore, when tuning CSS for performance, be aware that there are probably far better uses of time and effort in creating a faster webpage. To exemplify; optimizing a single image may well trump any optimizations you make to the entire CSS of a page.

Summary

We've covered a lot of ground in this chapter:

- How and when to use nesting
- How we can use nesting with the parent selector to work more easily with Modernizr
- How the `@extend` directive works
- What placeholder selectors are and how to use them
- How to use and write mixins to easily produce code on demand

As such, in this chapter we haven't made much of a dent in the design of `http://sassandcompass.com`.

However, the skills we've learnt are so useful in everything we're going to write in future; I think that's a fair trade-off.

It might take some time before you find yourself using these features day-to-day. Don't feel like you need to use them right away and at every available opportunity. If all you do for starters is nest and extend the odd style that's still progress, and it will make authoring style sheets easier than before. Once comfortable with that, when feeling feisty in the months to come (and if Compass doesn't already have a feature to solve the problem), maybe take a shot at writing a mixin or two.

In the next chapter, *Manipulate Color with Ease*, we're going to take a look at Sass and Compass's incredibly useful color functions. They will make working with color far easier; allowing colors to be transformed with simple commands such as lighten, darken, and saturate.

Manipulate Color with Ease

Hopefully by now, some of the Sass and Compass goodness is making sense. In the last chapter we learned how to split files into partials for convenience and better maintainability and looked at nesting, `@extend`, and placeholder selectors. We even have an understanding of mixins and what they do, even if we can't write them in our sleep yet.

This chapter is going to bring some of our existing skills together and add the incredible Sass and Compass color functions into the mix.

In this chapter, we will learn:

- How to convert a color from hex to RGBA
- How to darken and lighten colors
- How to saturate, desaturate, fade, and adjust the hue of color
- How to create inverted and complementary colors
- How to mix colors
- How to shade and tint colors
- How to combine color functions in a single statement

Throughout this chapter, we'll look in detail at the various color functions that Sass and Compass afford us and test them out on different sections of our test markup for `http://www.sassandcompass.com`.

Only define a color once

When working with Sass it's a perfectly reasonable aim to only define an individual color value once and then store it as a variable. The benefit of this approach is that if the color value needs to change, it only needs amending in one place, as it will propagate to all the necessary places on compile.

In the previous chapter, when making the testimonial module in the `_modules.scss` partial, instead of referencing a variable for a color value, a hex value was used. Following is some of that code:

```
.testimonial {
  background-color: #eee;
  border-top: 2px solid #ddd;
  border-bottom: 2px solid #ddd;
  padding: 1em 2em;
  ...more code...
}
```

There are two hex values being used in the preceding section, `#eee` and `#ddd`, and both are shades of gray (I'll resist the urge to insert a book pun here, oh wait). Instead of those hex values we will use the `lighten` color function of Sass to generate the colors from an existing color in the variables. Here are the colors currently defined in the `_variables.scss` partial:

```
$color1: #FF0000; // Red
$color2: #FFBF00; // Orange
$color3: #FFFF00; // Yellow
$color4: #7FFF00; // Green
$color5: #007FFF; // Light Blue
$color6: #00FFFF; // Cyan
$color7: #0000FF; // Blue
$color8: #7F00FF; // Purple
$color9: #FF00FF; // Magenta
$color10: #000; // Black
$color11: #FFF; // White
```

The variable naming conundrum

In this instance, variable names have been used that carry little to no semantic meaning. This is a double-edged sword. On the positive side, it means that if needed, different values can be assigned to each of the variables and the rest of the Sass files will still make sense.

To exemplify, if $color6 is used as a reference to a color, that still makes sense, regardless of what the color value is actually set to. However, if the variable was called $cyan and the value was changed to #FF0000, it would be more than a little confusing (as that hex value is red).

While naming color variables with arbitrary values solves one problem, the rub is that when writing styles, it's often necessary to keep checking what each variable represents (hence the comment next to each as a reminder of what each variable is currently set to). The danger is that doing that can slow down development and become a source of irritation.

One compromise between the two is to try and name the variables with intent. For example, $color-primary, $color-secondary, $color-tertiary, $color-primary-invert, and many more.

Sadly, there isn't a perfect solution. As with the practice of naming HTML classes, the most important thing is consistency and documentation. As long as you (and, if relevant, your team) have a documented and consistent approach, that's fine. Just use the way that works best for you.

The lighten and darken functions

The first two Sass color functions we will use are lighten and darken. As you might imagine, these lighten and darken an existing color using HSL color manipulations. Let's use lighten to amend an existing value and property pair. We will change the following code:

```
background-color: #eee;
```

To the following:

```
background-color: lighten($color10, 93.5%);
```

Instead of declaring the color itself, we are telling Sass 'lighten the value provided by 93.5 percent'. In this instance, the value being passed to the lighten function is the variable `$color10`. While the syntax may seem verbose (as opposed to simply writing the hex, RGB, or HSL value), it makes authoring far faster as it's possible to make quick alterations to colors without needing to touch Photoshop, Fireworks, and the like.

The `lighten` and `darken` functions can be used on any color. As the amendments happen with an HSL-based manipulation, Sass is actually increasing (with `lighten`) or decreasing (with `darken`) the amount of lightness in HSL color space and returning the amended color value as a hex value.

Understanding HSL colors

HSL works on a 360 degrees color wheel. Starting at the 12 o'clock position, yellow is at 60 degrees, green at 120 degrees, cyan at 180 degrees, blue at 240 degrees, magenta at 300 degrees, and finally red at 0 degrees. The first figure in an HSL color declaration (for example, `hsla(315, 100%, 50%, 1)`) represents Hue. So as the aforementioned HSL color had a hue of 315, it's easy to know that it will be between Magenta (at 300 degrees) and Red (at 0 degrees). The following two values are for saturation and lightness, specified as percentages, and these merely alter the base hue. Therefore, if wanting a more saturated or colorful appearance, use a higher percentage in the second value. The final value, controlling the lightness, can vary between 0 percent for black and 100 percent for white.

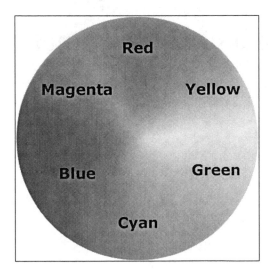

Syntax for lighten and darken

Let's break the Sass syntax down. First we write the `lighten` function, then open parenthesis:

```
lighten(
```

Then we pass the color we want to lighten and a comma:

```
lighten($color10,
```

Then the percentage we want to lighten the color, and then we close parenthesis:

```
lighten($color10, 93.5%)
```

It doesn't need to be a variable that's passed to the function. The same effect could be achieved as follows.

```
background-color: lighten(#000, 93.5%);
```

Either way, as expected, following is the CSS that is generated:

```
background-color: #eeeeee;
```

The `darken` function follows exactly the same syntax. Let's use it to amend the next color we have declared. Let's change the following code:

```
border-top: 2px solid #ddd;
```

To the following code:

```
border-top: 2px solid darken($color11, 13.5%);
```

Again, we are telling Sass, 'darken this color by 13.5 percent'. The color we are using in this instance is #FFF (the value assigned to `$color11`). As with all the color functions of Sass, we can pass a variable or a color value. Following is the generated CSS:

```
border-top: 2px solid #dddddd;
```

The Sass color functions can be used in a Sass file anywhere a color value would normally be declared in CSS. Tweaking colors, however, is then far easier as there's no need to open a color picker. For example, suppose the gray background needs to be just a little lighter. We can just amend the percentage accordingly:

```
background-color: lighten($color10, 95.5%);
```

Markup amendments and diversions

At this point, I'm aware that the markup of the test site won't easily let us achieve what I would like, design wise. Therefore, I'm going to make some amendments to the markup. For the sake of brevity, I won't bore you with the changes here. If you want to see exactly what changed, simply compare the code from this chapter and *Chapter 3, Nesting, Extend, Placeholders and Mixins*. However, here are just a few points of note.

A wrapping `div` element (each with class that begins with `inner`) is being added to the content inside the `<header>` and `<footer>` and a wrapping `div` tag around the main content and navigation areas. In the `_layout.scss` partial file, it has then allowed removal of the rules associated with the body tag, and instead we can add the following code:

```
[class ^="inner"] {
  max-width: 75em;
  margin: auto;
}
```

Incidentally, for those unaware what the `^` selector does, it targets all items that 'begin with' the value specified in quotation marks. There is also a substring selector for 'contains' (using the `*` symbol) and 'ends with' (using the `$` symbol). More information on these CSS level 3 substring selectors can be found at `http://www.w3.org/TR/selectors/#attribute-substrings`. They are also quite well supported (IE7+ and all modern browsers).

This means that the three extra `div` elements added to the markup that all begin with `inner` will have a maximum width of 75em and an even margin either side (to center them).

Why ems?

There are all manner of units that can be used on widths: **em**, **rem**, **px** and **percentage**, for example. We're moving to ems here rather than pixels for the max-width value, as it will then tie more closely to the content (which is almost exclusively text). It will also make things more flexible when we look at changing the layout for different viewports in *Chapter 6, Advanced Media Queries with Sass*.

The Compass clearfix

Chances are, if you're reading a book about Sass and Compass, you already know what a CSS **clearfix** is. However, for the sake of completeness: it's CSS that needs adding to an element if it's floated within another block level element that doesn't have a float value declared. Because using the float property removes an element from the flow, it looks, visually, like it's broken out of its container.

Without Sass and Compass, it's standard practice to add an HTML class like .clearfix or .group to elements in the markup (with the necessary corresponding clearfix code in the CSS) that need it.

Using Sass and Compass, it's possible to have clearfixes wherever they are needed without littering our code with HTML classes purely for the purpose of a clearfix.

In the amended code, certain rules have had a clearfix mixin included. Ordinarily, the Compass clearfix mixin is added as follows:

```
@include clearfix;
```

The clearfix relevant part of CSS generated by the mixin is as follows:

```
overflow: hidden;
*zoom: 1;
```

Things can be improved even more. Rather than include the clearfix mixin on any other rule that needs it, we can make a placeholder selector for it and then extend it.

That will mean any future selectors that need clearfix code will get added into a single combined selector rather than have repeated clearfix code in every rule that needs it.

There's an argument that extending singular CSS hacks with a placeholder style in this manner can make the code less portable. That's certainly true if you'll be handing the generated CSS to someone else to work on. The reason being that they will need the style for the selector and the combined selector that includes the selector with the clearfix too. Just something to be aware of before extending properties in this manner.

If you need to generate CSS for someone else to work with afterwards, or if you'd prefer all styles relevant to a selector in one place, just include the mixin rather than extending it.

Let's do that now. Create a `_placeholders.scss` partial file and then add the following code:

```scss
%clearfix {
  @include clearfix;
}
```

Then ensure the new partial is imported into the main `styles.scss` file:

```scss
@import "compass";
@import "partials/variables";
@import "partials/mixins";
@import "partials/fonts";
@import "partials/normalize";
@import "partials/base";
@import "partials/placeholders";
@import "partials/layout";
@import "partials/modules";
```

Now, when any element requires a clearfix, we can just use the following code:

```scss
@extend %clearfix;
```

With this method, the clearfix relevant styles get separated out to their own rule. This might seem counter-intuitive; however, the more elements that need the clearfix rules, the more economical the approach will be. For example, the following code shows another three elements to illustrate what happens:

```scss
.clearfix-please {
  @extend %clearfix;
}
.ooh-clearfix-here-too {
  @extend %clearfix;
}
.and-me {
  @extend %clearfix;
}
```

This means a rule such as the following code is generated in the CSS:

```css
.clearfix-please, .ooh-clearfix-here-too, .and-me {
  overflow: hidden;
  *zoom: 1;
}
```

This isn't essential practice by any means (and in the preceding tip a counter argument is provided), but the larger the project, the greater the likely advantages.

Back to colors

Right, back to colors. Let's bring together a few of the techniques we have learnt in this and previous chapters to convert the top links (currently sitting on the right-hand side of the header area) into buttons.

We will create a mixin that will let us easily create button variations, providing various foreground and background colors. As ever, when writing a custom mixin, the pay off is greater the more often the job needs repeating. In our little site, it's arguably not worth the bother, but the technique is worth understanding for that occasion when multiple yet varied versions of a similar style are required.

The `_mixins.scss` partial is where the following code will be added.

Don't be alarmed, the following code might look like gibberish, but it will make sense shortly:

```
@mixin button-links($button-base: darken($color11,10%),$button-hover:
darken($color11,15%)) {
  border: 1px solid darken($color11,16%);
  padding: .3em .6em;
  margin-left: .7em;
  @include border-radius(8px);
  @include text-shadow(0 1px 2px $color11);
   color: lighten($color10,50%);
  background-color: $button-base;
  &:hover {
    background-color: $button-hover;
  }
}
```

Then back in the `_modules.scss` file, the following code is being added to the header styles:

```
.main-link {
  @include button-links;
}
```

The preceding code produces the following screenshot in the browser:

How does that code actually work? First, let's take a look at the mixin again and then break it down:

```
@mixin button-links($button-base: darken($color11,10%),$button-hover:
darken($color11,15%)) {
  border: 1px solid darken($color11,16%);
  padding: .3em .6em;
  margin-left: .7em;
  @include border-radius(8px);
  @include text-shadow(0 1px 2px $color11);
   color: lighten($color10,50%);
  background-color: $button-base;
  &:hover {
    background-color: $button-hover;
  }
}
```

First, the mixin is named `button-links`:

```
@mixin button-links(
```

Then, after opening the parenthesis, a couple of default arguments are set:

```
@mixin button-links($button-base: darken($color11,10%),$button-hover:
darken($color11,15%)) {
```

There's one argument called `$button-base` with the default value of the variable `$color11` (which has a value of `#FFF`/white) darkened by 10 percent. Then, after a comma, another argument called `$button-hover`, which has the default value of the variable `$color11` darkened by 15 percent.

These keywords are then placed at various points in the enclosed mixin code so that whatever is entered when including the mixin gets placed where it needs to. We'll look at that again in a moment, but for now, have you noticed that within this *home-made* mixin there are also another couple of mixins:

```
@include border-radius(8px);
@include text-shadow(0 1px 2px $color11);
```

Mixins within mixins? What is this new devilry?

These two mixins are actually another two existing Compass mixins. As we've already established, Compass has a raft of predefined mixins that make authoring style sheets easier. In particular, Compass makes writing styles to support CSS level 3 features in browsers really easy, and we'll cover a lot of those in greater detail in *Chapter 7, Easy CSS3, Image Sprites, and More with Compass*.

For now, we'll just incorporate a couple more Compass mixins that produce CSS you are probably familiar with: border-radius and text-shadow. In the first mixin, the argument being passed is the border-radius value (in pixels). With the text-shadow mixin, the values are the horizontal offset, the vertical offset, the blur (all in pixels), and then the color.

The rest of the mixin should be more straightforward to understand; using variables for colors and the lighten color function. The mixin itself is then included in the _modules.scss file:

```
.main-link {
  @include button-links;
}
```

With the defaults used, following is the CSS code the mixin generates:

```
header .main-link {
  border: 1px solid #d6d6d6;
  padding: .3em .6em;
  margin-left: .7em;
  -webkit-border-radius: 8px;
  -moz-border-radius: 8px;
  -ms-border-radius: 8px;
  -o-border-radius: 8px;
  border-radius: 8px;
  text-shadow: 0 1px 2px white;
  color: gray;
  background-color: #e6e6e6;
}
header .main-link:hover {
  background-color: #d9d9d9;
}
```

You can see that the `border-radius` mixin also generates a full vendor-prefixed set of property/value pairs for different browser vendors for optimum browser compatibility.

Considering the actual output, creating that mixin may initially seem like a lot of work. However, remember that it will earn its keep the more often it is used, whether in this project or future ones.

We now have a button mixin that we can pass arguments to. Remember, the first value is the standard background color, the second is the background color on hover. We can pass actual color values or variables. For example:

```
.main-link {
  @include button-links($color2,$color3);
}
```

As `$color2` is an orange color and `$color3` is a yellow, we get buttons that have an orange background and then a yellow background when hovered over. The following screenshot shows how they render in the browser:

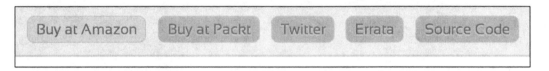

It's at this point that people reading this on a color e-book reader have a distinct advantage over those reading the printed version (sadly grayscale only).

If the colors aren't exactly what's needed it's also possible to pass colors to the mixin as Sass's color functions:

```
.main-link {
  @include button-links(complement(lighten($color9,48%)),complement
  (lighten($color9,40%)));
}
```

This is another piece of code that, admittedly, looks intimidating. Especially given the abundance of parentheses.

To make matters easier, use variables

I don't mind seeing color functions littered throughout the code. I actually prefer it that way, as it enables me to easily tweak values whilst developing. However, I'll also be the first to admit that it can get pretty messy looking.

For cleaner looking code, consider creating new variables for the color functions. For example, instead of the mixin as in the preceding code, do this:

```
$btn-mint: complement(lighten($color9,48%));
$btn-mint-hover: complement(lighten($color9,40%));
.main-link {
  @include button-links($btn-mint,$btn-mint-hover);
}
```

In this example, we've made new variables for the color conversions and then passed those new variables to the mixin (instead of the color functions themselves).

The only new thing however, is the **complement** color function. Let's break the code down and then we'll look at complement in greater detail.

First of all, we include the mixin and open a parenthesis. Then we pass in the arguments (remember, there is one for the background color and another for the background color on hover):

```
@include button-links(
```

We're passing the first color value as an argument. However, rather than merely passing a variable or a hex value as we have previously, we're actually passing a color function. We are effectively saying to Sass, "Produce a color that is complementary to $color9 after it has been lightened 48 percent". Here's how that looks in code:

```
@include button-links(complement(lighten($color9,48%))
```

Those parentheses work exactly as they do in math equations and the dreaded Microsoft Excel. They enclose a piece of arithmetic. I'm a math dunce myself, so if it looks confusing, just remember that if a parenthesis opens in a rule, it must also close somewhere else, otherwise you'll see an error.

Now we want to pass the next argument to the mixin, the one that will generate the hover color. We use a comma (to separate the two arguments) and then include the next argument. As before, it's not merely a color value or variable, it's a color function. Following is the second argument in isolation:

```
complement(lighten($color9,40%))
```

That's effectively telling Sass that the second color should be "a complementary color of the variable $color9 after it has been lightened by 40 percent". Following is the full mixin again, hopefully making a little more sense than it did at first:

```
@include button-links(complement(lighten($color9,48%)),complement
(lighten($color9,40%)));
```

The following code is the generated CSS:

```
header .main-link {
  border: 1px solid #d6d6d6;
  padding: .3em .6em;
  margin-left: .7em;
  -webkit-border-radius: 8px;
  -moz-border-radius: 8px;
  -ms-border-radius: 8px;
  -o-border-radius: 8px;
  border-radius: 8px;
  text-shadow: 0 1px 2px white;
  color: gray;
  background-color: #f5fff5;
}
header .main-link:hover {
  background-color: #ccffcc;
}
```

And here's a screenshot showing the result in the browser:

I'm still not thrilled with that look. However, we can fix that up with a little CSS3 goodness in *Chapter 7, Easy CSS3, Image Sprites, and More with Compass*. For now, let's learn about more Sass and Compass color functions.

The complement (and invert) functions

We just used the complement color function in our mixin. It takes a color value and then computes a value that is 180 degrees opposite on the HSL color wheel. Let's add a background color to our chapter lists on the website and then test complement and other Sass and Compass color functions out:

```
.chapter-summary {
  &:nth-child(1) a {
    background-color: $color1;
  }
  &:nth-child(2) a {
    background-color: complement($color1);
  }
}
```

In this example, the first list item link is getting a background value of red (that's what the variable $color1 is set to) and the second list item link is getting a background color that is a complementary color of that. Here's the generated CSS:

```
.chapter-summary:nth-child(1) a {
  background-color: red;
}
.chapter-summary:nth-child(2) a {
  background-color: cyan;
}
```

In the absence of nth-child

In this section we're using the nth-child pseudo selector to target the list item links. However, nth-child isn't universally supported; IE8 and below being notable examples (http://caniuse. com/#feat=css-sel3). When wider support is needed, consider using the attribute selector. That will get you support in IE7 and IE8 but not IE6:

```
[href^="chapter1"]
```

The following screenshot shows the result of those rules in the browser:

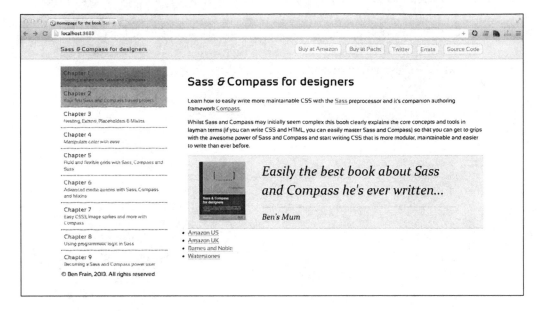

The invert function

The `invert` function is very similar to `complement`, and the two can be used interchangeably in many practical situations. However, be aware there is a subtle difference; `invert` provides the inverted red, green, and blue values of a color, leaving opacity as it is.

The adjust-hue function

The `adjust-hue` function can produce exactly the same effect as complement:

```
background-color: adjust-hue($color1, 180deg);
```

However, with `adjust-hue`, it's possible to vary the color produced by varying the degree of hue (it can be a positive or negative value). Let's use this on the third list item:

```
background-color: adjust-hue($color1, 90deg);
```

Here is the generated CSS:

```
.chapter-summary:nth-child(3) a {
  background-color: #80ff00;
}
```

The following screenshot shows what that gives us in the browser:

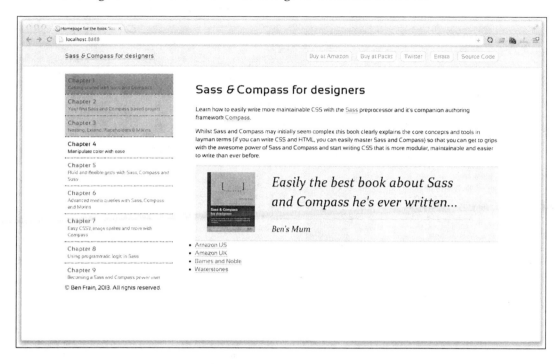

The `adjust-hue` function can be applied to any color value. It can accept a degree range from 0 to 360 (in CSS the degree is written as `20deg` or `290deg` for example).

The saturate and desaturate functions

The `saturate` and `desaturate` functions adjust the saturation value for a color. Let's use this to create a color for our next list item:

```
&:nth-child(4) a {
  background-color: desaturate($color1, 80%);
}
```

Here is how that compiles in CSS:

```
.chapter-summary:nth-child(4) a {
  background-color: #996666;
}
```

And the following screenshot shows our fourth list item in the browser (note that the dotted borders on the list items have been removed at this point for clarity):

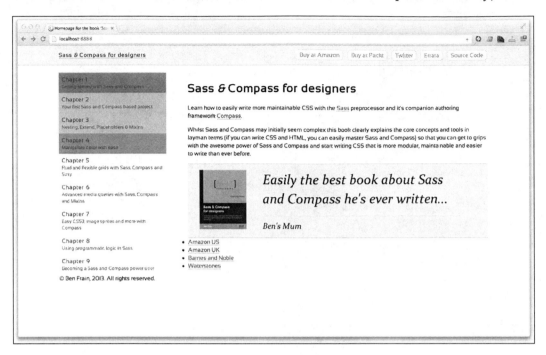

The `saturate` function increases the saturation level of a color. We'll use it on the fifth list item along with a hex value instead of a variable (just because we can):

```
&:nth-child(5) a {
  background-color: saturate(#996666, 40%);
}
```

The following screenshot shows it in the browser:

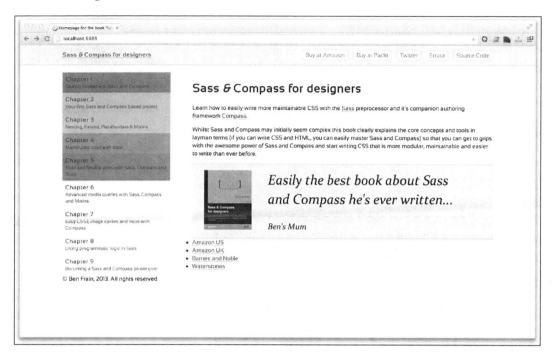

The transparentize/fade-out functions

Need to create a color with an alpha channel? Just tell Sass how transparent it needs to be and it will do the heavy lifting. The best bit is that you don't even need to pass Sass a color value that already has an alpha channel. It will transform the color into an RGBA value for you. Let's use the `transparentize` function on the sixth list item:

```
&:nth-child(6) a {
  background-color: transparentize($color1, .5);
}
```

After passing the color, the `transparentize` function expects a value between 0 (entirely transparent) and 1 (entirely opaque). Here we are using `.5`.

 `fade-out` can be used instead of `transparentize` if you would rather, as it has the same effect. The `rgba` function also shares similarities, more of which shortly.

Now, remember, `$color1` has a hex color as its value (`#FF0000`), and yet on compile, this is what the function produces for us in CSS:

```
.chapter-summary:nth-child(6) a {
   background-color: rgba(255, 0, 0, 0.5);
}
```

A color value defined as RGBA. Sass, you are too good to us, you really are. No more color pickers, external color conversion utilities, and the like; Sass and Compass can do all the color conversions we need, right in the code!

The opacify/fade-in functions

The `opacify` and `fade-in` do the exact opposite of `transparentize`/`fade-out`. It makes a color more opaque. Here are two examples of the syntax for reference. One uses `fade-in`, the other uses `opacify`, both have exactly the same effect:

```
background-color: fade-in($color3, .3);
background-color: opacify($color3, .3);
```

The grayscale function

Treat yourself to a cookie if you can guess what the `grayscale` function does. Yep, it converts the color passed to it into a grayscale color. Not much more to say really:

```
&:nth-child(7) a {
   background-color: grayscale($color1);
}
```

Following is the output on the browser:

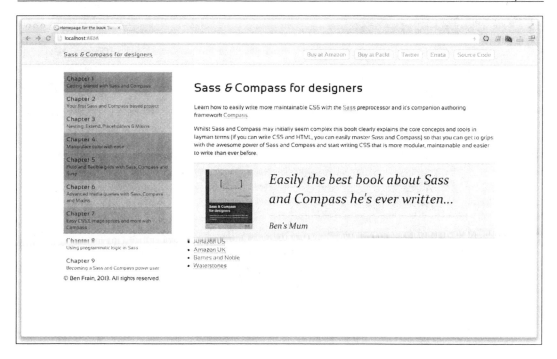

The rgba function

If you want to convert an existing color value (defined as either a variable or hex value) to an RGBA value (including an alpha layer for transparency), use the `rgba` function:

```
background-color: rgba(red,.9);
```

This will produce following CSS:

```
background-color: rgba(255, 0, 0, 0.9);
```

The two arguments needed are the color and then the value of the alpha layer (`0` is entirely transparent, `1` is entirely opaque, `.5` is halfway between the two).

From a practical point of view, it's similar to `transparentize`/`fade-out` and `opacify`/`fade-in`.

 Be aware that unless the value passed for the alpha layer is less than `1`, Sass will compile the resultant color as a hex value or a named CSS color.

The mix function

You can mix two colors together in Sass using the `mix` function. Let's use the mix function for the eighth list item link:

```
&:nth-child(8) a {
  background-color: mix($color1,$color2,60%);
}
```

Here's how the syntax works. First, after defining the function and opening the parenthesis, we pass two color values separated by a comma. As with all the color functions, you can use actual values or a variable. Then, after a second comma, we specify the weight of the mix.

The weight value is used to specify how much of the first color is mixed in with the second. In our preceding example, we are mixing in 60 percent of red (#FF0000 as defined in the variable $color1) into orange (#FFBF00 as defined in the variable $color2).

The following code is the resultant CSS:

```
.chapter-summary:nth-child(8) a {
  background-color: #ff4c00;
}
```

As you might imagine, in the browser it produces a very reddish-orange:

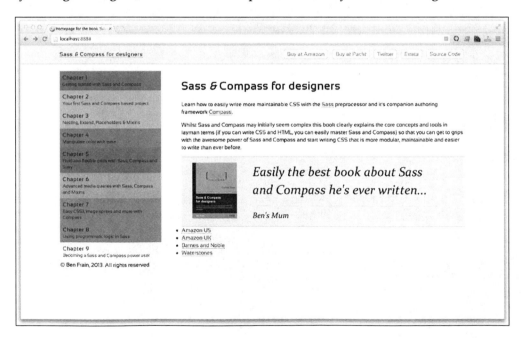

The adjust-color function

The `adjust-color` function allows manipulation of any color property. It's possible to adjust the red, green, and blue (properties that make up colors in RGB color space) or the hue, saturation, or lightness of a color (properties that make up colors in HSL color space). The alpha layer of a color can also be adjusted. It's not the simplest color function, but it does provide an amazing amount of granularity.

Each adjustable color property has a relevant keyword argument:

- `$red, $green, $blue`: The values for red, green, and blue should be a number between `0` and `255`
- `$hue`: The hue value should be a plus or minus number for degrees on a color wheel between `0` and `359`
- `$saturation, $lightness`: Saturation and lightness should be a percentage as a plus or minus between `0` and `100`
- `$alpha`: A number between 0 and 1

That's a lot to take in, so let's consider some examples:

```
background-color: adjust-color($color1, $hue:40);
```

The preceding code takes the color and adjusts the hue property by 40 degrees.

```
background-color: adjust-color($color1, $hue:40, $lightness: 20);
```

The preceding example adjusts the hue by 40 degrees and also adjusts the lightness of the color by 20 percent.

```
background-color: adjust-color($color1, $red:40, $green: 20);
```

The preceding example adjusts the red property to 40 and the green to 20.

```
background-color: adjust-color($color1, $red:40, $hue: 20);
```

The preceding example will produce an error: **Cannot specify HSL and RGB values for a color at the same time for `adjust-color`**.

Be aware that when using the `adjust-color` function you must limit adjustments to either HSL or RGB at one time.

The scale-color function

The prior `adjust-color` changes a color by a set amount; `scale-color` on the other hand adjusts a color by an amount based upon what it already is. That will make more sense if we look at a few examples.

Let's remove the prior list item colors and leave just the first one as red (set by the variable `$color1`).

Now let's add two further rules for the following two list item links, one using `adjust-color` and the final one using `scale-color`. However, notice that the same numerical value is being passed to each color function to demonstrate the difference:

```
&:nth-child(1) a {
  background-color: $color1;
}
&:nth-child(2) a {
  background-color: adjust-color($color1,$lightness:-20%);
}
&:nth-child(3) a {
  background-color: scale-color($color1,$lightness:-20%);
}
```

Following is the CSS generated by that Sass:

```
.chapter-summary:nth-child(1) a {
  background-color: red;
}
.chapter-summary:nth-child(2) a {
  background-color: #990000;
}
.chapter-summary:nth-child(3) a {
  background-color: #cc0000;
}
```

And following is the result in the browser:

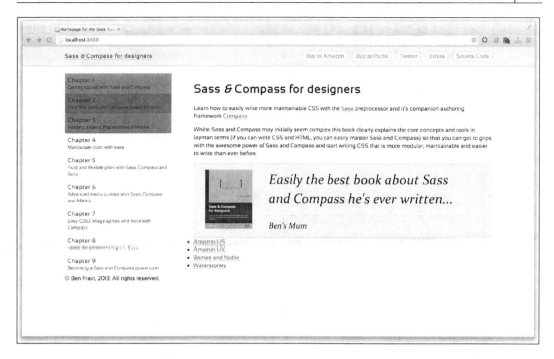

The `adjust-color` function has taken the red color and reduced the lightness by a fixed 20 percent.

The `scale-color` function on the other hand has considered how light the red color already is and then made a `1` to `100` scale from that point to complete lightness. It has then moved (scaled) the color 20 percent along that scale.

For more on the Sass and Compass color functions, I'd recommend checking out the documentation on the Sass website at `http://sass-lang.com/docs/yardoc/Sass/Script/Functions.html` and the documentation on the Compass web site at `http://compass-style.org/reference/compass/helpers/colors/`.

The shade and tint functions

Compass has another two functions you might find handy: `shade` and `tint`. The `shade` function mixes the color with a percentage of black while `tint` mixes the color with a percentage of white. Let's adjust the fourth and fifth list item links with these two functions:

```
&:nth-child(4) a {
  background-color: shade($color1,60%);
}
&:nth-child(5) a {
  background-color: tint($color1,60%);
}
```

The following screenshot shows what that produces in the browser:

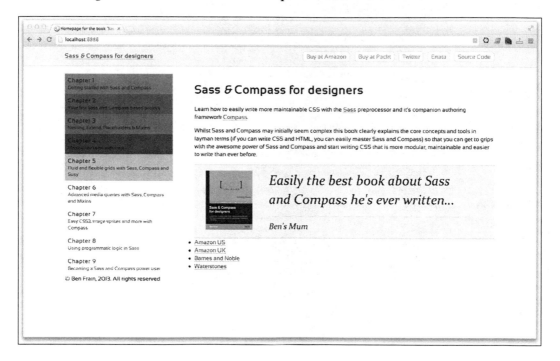

These two functions are handy when it comes to converting graphics composites where designers have added *highlight* and *lowlight* lines. Often this is achieved in Photoshop and Fireworks by adding thin lines of white or black and then using transparency to fade them over a background color. When applied to a color value that would be the color underneath the highlight line in the graphics application, the `tint` and `shade` functions will produce an equivalent color value in the browser.

Putting it all together

We've already combined color functions in the earlier mixin near the beginning of this chapter. However, the process for combining functions perhaps bears repeating with an example.

Need a `0.7` alpha layer on an RGBA color that's a 30 percent mix of two colors? The following code describes how you'd do that:

```
&:nth-child(9) a {
  background-color: rgba((mix($color1,$color2,60%)),.7);
}
```

And the following screenshot is the result in the browser (note that, a repeating background image has been added to the body to demonstrate the alpha channel of the color):

Chapter 9
Becoming a Sass and Compass power user

The syntax for combining color functions does look intimidating at first, but once you've started to adjust colors in this manner you'll find it saves a lot of time. No need to open color pickers. Instead, with Sass and Compass, we can test colors directly in the browser.

Subtle background patterns

Want a great subtle background pattern for your site design? Look no further than `http://www.subtlepatterns.com`. This site provides free patterns that in most cases even include a double-size version for use on high-resolution displays. Not sure how to incorporate high-resolution images? Look no further than this blog post at `http://benfra.in/1xs`.

Summary

A look at our test web page at this point would indicate that all we have achieved in this chapter is to produce a list of gaudy-colored links (as such, I've moved our color function examples into a partial file called `_chapter-examples.scss`).

However, more important than the result is the knowledge of Sass and Compass's color functions. We now understand how we can mix, alter, and transparentize colors and create inversions, complements, and adjustments of any color at will.

Before we address the ugliness of our site (of which I am acutely aware), there's still the actual layout of the site to sort out.

Grids are obviously perfect for this task. However, historically, popular CSS-based grid frameworks like Blueprint and 960 have necessitated adding extra classes in the markup. That's always felt a little *off* to me. It certainly isn't the most semantic way of marking up content.

Thankfully, adding HTML classes in the markup to create a grid system simply isn't needed with Sass and Compass. In the next chapter we're going to look at Sass and Compass grid systems. They will let us create our own fluid, flexible, and responsive grids with ease.

5
Responsive and Flexible Grids with Sass and Compass

The use of grids for visual layout is a technique that dates back hundreds of years. Pick up any newspaper and you can see a grid at work. Its principal aim is to bring visual harmony to possible discord. A great grid structure can bind columns of type, the media within them, the headings above them, and more. At the risk of being reductive, a grid helps provide some relationship between the component parts of a layout.

 Although we will consider Sass and Compass tools for building a grid in this chapter, the fundamentals of creating grids and how to establish relationships between elements is beyond my expertise, so I'd therefore recommend taking a look at this round up of resources at *Smashing Magazine*: http://www.smashingmagazine. com/2007/04/14/designing-with-grid-based-approach/.

When tasked with building a website from a graphical composite, it's possible you'll be building a grid system without even realizing it. A good designer will have sweated over the relationships between all the visual elements and will have possibly employed a grid system to structure those relationships. As the composite is built out, the grid is recreated in code.

Without a graphical composite as a starting point, a grid can be even more useful. It can provide a framework to hang visual components on. This chapter is all about exploring Sass and Compass tools and the techniques that make working with grid systems simpler.

In this chapter, we will cover:

- Reasons you might want to use a grid system
- The benefits of using a Sass and Compass based grid
- Installing the Susy grid system plugin
- Including Susy in a Compass-based project
- Setting up a Susy grid for a responsive 'mobile first' design
- Creating example grid layouts
- Creating a completely fluid grid
- Creating a static 'fixed' grid
- Understanding the core Susy grid helpers
- Sub-pixel rounding woes and Susy helpers

Arguments against grids

Grids are a divisive topic. As useful as they can be, there are a few common complaints with them. Let's deal with these first.

Semantic purists argue that writing markup laden with HTML classes such as `column_8` and `column_4` is tantamount to a cardinal sin. Let's squash this issue right away; using Sass and Compass based grids requires zero amendments to the markup.

Another common objection is that starting a design with a grid system stifles creativity, imposing an artificial construct before more critical design decisions have (or should have) been made. If that is a sentiment you agree with, I would offer this olive branch; when using Sass and Compass the grid system need not be pre-defined or pre-prescribed.

What we will be working with is a truly flexible grid system that can be implemented at any time during the design and build of a website. Make the design however you want, then use Sass and Compass to build out that design with relative ease. Have as many columns as you need, use whatever unit of measurement you like and even nest grids within other grids. If that isn't good enough, this grid system creates responsive-friendly layouts so the site will display peachy on any device.

Reasons to use a grid system

The main reason Sass and Compass based grid systems are great to work with is that they handle all the complex mathematics. Hands up who enjoys working out the percentage calculations necessary for layouts? I know I can live without that and a Sass and Compass based grid system allows us to deal with layouts in a less academic manner. They do this by using mixin names that abstract some of the complexities of widths into simpler terms. But we are perhaps getting ahead of ourselves. Let me first tell you a little about the first Sass and Compass based grid system I fell in love with.

What is Susy?

There are a number of Sass and Compass grid systems available. Everyone has their favorite and mine is **Susy**. It's simple to use, produces clean code and is extremely flexible and well documented. See the boxout section for information on some others but understand that for this chapter we will chiefly be working with Susy (because it's been scientifically tested to be 99.99% amazing*).

Susy was principally created by Eric A. Meyer (not to be confused with the 'CSS reset' Eric A. Meyer), a core member of the Compass team.

I mention this for two reasons, firstly, by way of a hat tip to him and secondly, to let you know that you are in safe hands. Susy works beautifully with Sass and Compass projects and I find it the easiest way to build responsive grids.

There are plenty of other grid systems for Sass and Compass we won't be looking at. If Susy doesn't do it for you (seriously, what is wrong with you?), consider looking at Zen Grids (http://zengrids.com) or the one that comes as part of the Sass and Compass framework Foundation 3 by Zurb: http://foundation.zurb.com.

Alternatively, consider the Flex Grid that comes with the Sass mixin library Bourbon: http://thoughtbot.com/bourbon/#flex-grid or the Salsa grid system: http://tsi.github.com/Salsa.

You may even choose to 'roll your own' Sass and Compass grid system. Everything needed is certainly available. However, the complexities of doing so are beyond the scope of this book and your humble author's capabilities.

*No scientific tests were actually performed; you'll just have to take my word for it.

The homepage for Susy is `http://susy.oddbird.net/`. There are tutorials and reference documentation there galore! In fact, rather than merely repeat all the documentation available there, in this chapter, I want to concentrate on showing you what can be achieved with Susy by applying it to our existing site design to create a 'mobile first' responsive layout.

Modular scale and Vertical rhythm

Susy principally deals with widths and alignment on a horizontal axis. If you're looking for something to help create efficient vertical rhythm, be aware that Compass has its own vertical rhythm tools. Here is the official documentation: `http://compass-style.org/reference/compass/typography/vertical_rhythm/`. I'll be the first to admit, however, that the Compass docs on this can seem a little impenetrable. A good beginner tutorial on the subject can be found here: `http://atendesigngroup.com/blog/vertical-rhythm-compass`.

Typography geeks will be thrilled to know this can be taken still further by using the Compass Modular scale plugin (`https://github.com/scottkellum/modular-scale`) to create a modular scale that can then be applied using Compass's vertical rhythm tools.

What does Susy actually do?

Before we start using Susy to build our grids, it is perhaps worth making it clear that from a conceptual point of view, Susy facilitates making grids. It does not actually *make them for us*. That's our job!

Let me expand on that a little. Susy allows us to define what we want building and then it does all the complex calculations. In layman's terms, at a basic level it allows one to say, "I want a grid that's 12 columns wide, each column should be `5em` wide with a `1em` gutter and `1em` of padding on either side of the grid". Then Susy makes the calculations to make that work. As ever, hopefully this distinction will make more sense when we start using it, so let's get stuck in.

If you're not already familiar with responsive web design, at this point, I'd direct you towards my earlier book, *Responsive Web Design with HTML5 and CSS3* (get it here: `http://benfra.in/1y5`)—not just to line my pockets, although obviously I won't be complaining, but because many of the conventions we'll discuss in this chapter and the next relate to responsive web design, something that can't be sufficiently summarized here.

Installing the Susy Compass plugin

As some GUI Sass compiler tools include Susy and some don't, we will err on the side of caution and install Susy from the command line. Susy is another plugin and like the other Sass and Compass based goodies we have dealt with, they are available as gems that we can install from the command line.

Open up your command-line tool ('Command Prompt with Ruby' on Windows, 'Terminal' or 'iTerm' on OS X) and enter the following command:

```
gem install susy
```

Remember if you are running OS X you may need to prefix the command with `sudo`:

```
sudo gem install susy
```

Enter your usual desktop password if prompted and press *Enter*.

> Remember the command line won't give you any visual indication that the password is being input, you'll likely just see the cursor blinking in the same position.

You should see a response like this once installed:

Fetching: susy-1.0.7.gem (100%)

Successfully installed susy-1.0.7

1 gem installed

Well done, you just installed another Ruby gem; you are getting good at this!

> If using CodeKit, it's possible that to get Susy working you may need to link to your system's (not CodeKit's) own version of Sass and Compass. In this instance, try the following:
>
> **Option 1**: In CodeKit, open **Preferences | Languages** and then Sass and then under **Advanced Compiler Settings**, click **Use the Sass executable at this path** and browse to `/usr/bin/sass`. Then do the same for Compass (**Advanced Compiler Settings**, and choose `/usr/bin/compass`).
>
> **Option 2**: Change the path to Susy in your `config.rb` file. So, for example, use this instead:
>
> ```
> require "/Library/Ruby/Gems/1.8/gems/susy-1.0.7"
> ```

Including Susy in a project

Back in *Chapter 2, Setting Up a Sass and Compass project*, we looked at how the
config.rb file allows us to specify any required plugins. We need to ensure that
our project 'knows' that we require Susy. Open the config.rb file and enter the
following line at the top (if it is not there already):

```
require "susy"
```

> You can also create a blank project with Susy using the following
> command (where project-name is the name of the project you
> wish to create):
>
> ```
> compass create project-name -r susy -u susy
> ```
>
> This will create a Compass-based project including files such as
> a _base.scss partial that already contains the required variables
> and imports them to get started with a Susy layout.

Now our project knows we need Susy, we need to actually include it in our project.

Susy project variables

Susy uses a number of variables to define the settings of a grid. When creating a
Susy project from scratch (see the previous tip), Susy places these variables in the
_base.scss file. However, in the site we are building, we are adding anything
related to the structural layout into the _layout.scss partial file. At present,
this is the content of that partial file:

```
* {
  @include bs;
}
[class^="inner"] {
  max-width: 75em;
  margin: auto;
}
header[role="banner"],footer[role="contentinfo"] {
  width: 100%;
  display: block;
}
nav[role="navigation"] {
  width: 25%;
  float: left;
}
```

```
.main-content {
  width: 70%;
  float: right;
}
footer[role="contentinfo"] {
  clear: both;
}
```

Currently, it's a very simple layout that only works acceptably on desktop size viewports (say 1000px plus). Let's trash this.

Instead, we will replace that layout with a fully responsive layout that works at viewports from handhelds all the way to large desktop screens. We will use Susy to achieve this goal.

First, let's set Susy up, then apply some of its goodness.

Setting up a Susy grid

When setting up a Susy grid, the first thing we will do is include all the necessary Susy-specific variables for the grid. Let's add the following at the top of the _layout. scss partial:

```
@import "susy";
$total-columns   : 12;              // a 12-column grid
$column-width    : 5em;             // each column is 5em wide
$gutter-width    : 1em;             // 1em gutters between columns
$grid-padding    : $gutter-width;   // grid-padding equal to gutters
```

First, we are importing Susy using the @import directive and then defining some settings for a grid as values next to the various Susy variables. Let's look at each of these:

- $total-columns: This is the number of columns we want our grid to have. Here we are using a 12-column grid but it can be any number of columns you like.

- $column-width: This is the width of each column in the grid. We are using em as a unit of measurement here but it could be defined as pixels if you would rather; Susy won't mind.

- $gutter-width: Defines the amount of space between each column. For starters, we are using 1em.

- $grid-padding: Is the space at either side of the grid. At present, it is set to be equal to the gutter width but it does not have to be.

Defining a context for the grid

At this point, nothing has changed. We have just imported Susy and defined the settings but we are not actually using it. To use it, we need to set one or more elements as a container element (the 'context' for grid columns).

The importance of context

Context is an important concept to grasp when working with Susy. The context is simply the containing element for grid items. Perhaps more importantly, the number of columns that the containing element spans. For the most part, in our example we are dealing with a 12-column grid and no nesting, so the context is usually 12. However, if things start going screwy when working with grid elements, ensure you're not inadvertently nesting a grid item within a new context. For example, if an element within a grid is also set as a container it becomes the context for any elements nested within it.

Let's therefore amend the first section of the existing layout rules to this:

```
[class^="inner"] {
  @include container;
}
```

Instead of specifying an actual width for these elements (remember this selector applies to all elements with a class beginning with `inner`), we just told Susy that each of them is a `container`, a context for grid columns to live within. We have done this by including the `container` mixin. Susy then magically computes what size they should be in relation to the variables defined for the grid. Having included that `container` mixin, here is what we get in the browser:

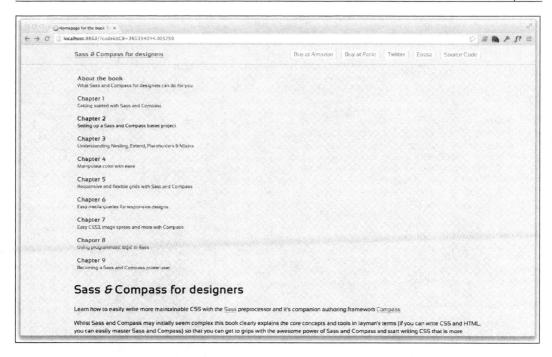

We have a context for our grid but nothing within it defined so we just have all the elements filling their default space. This may seem like a step backwards but trust me, this is progress.

Showing the grid background

Although we can't see the grid actually working, thankfully, Susy can show us! One thing that is particularly useful when setting up a grid using Susy, is the ability to show the grid columns in the browser for each container. Let's amend the rule to this:

```
[class^="inner"] {
  @include container;
  @include susy-grid-background;
}
```

And this is what we now see in the background:

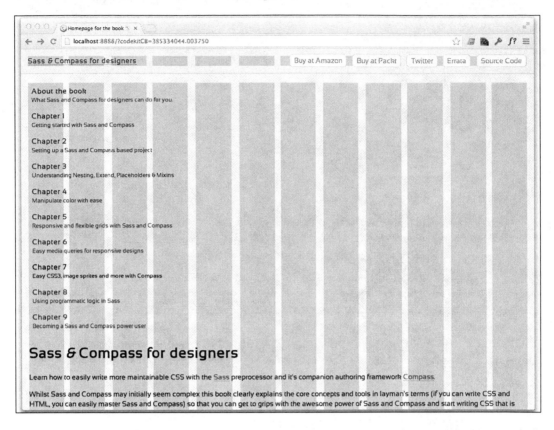

Nice! We've added the `susy-grid-background` mixin to the containers and that produces a CSS background gradient on those elements so we can see the columns in the browser. Now we can easily see where content is aligning based upon our grid.

Setting Susy to border-box

Before we go any further, let's tell Susy that we are using the `border-box` box-sizing model as this affects the way padding and borders work with the columns. We can do this by adding this variable below the other grid settings:

```
$border-box-sizing: true;
```

If we hadn't already set the box-sizing model to `border-box` on every element (remember we made a mixin for this in *Chapter 3, Nesting, Extend, Placeholders, and Mixins*), we could effectively kill two birds with one stone by using the following Susy mixin instead of adding the previous variable:

```
@include border-box-sizing;
```

Making a 'mobile first' responsive grid

When building up a responsive design, the initial layout I think about is what I consider the 'accessibility' layout. The idea of this is that no matter the device or capability (crucially, whether or not JavaScript is supported on the device) this layout should work and provide access to the content. It doesn't need to be the 'optimum' visual layout. For example, the chapter lists will need scrolling past before each page's main content, but it will still be accessible.

Having looked at the design, perhaps we can get away with just three visual **breakpoints** for the design structure (a 'breakpoint' merely being a term used to specify where the layout should change based upon available space in the viewport).

 Viewport is a term used to describe (and distinguish) the viewable size of a browser window from the size of the device screen itself. On a smartphone, the size of the viewport is typically the same as the device window (sans interface 'chrome'). However, on laptops and desktops, the browser window can be resized, allowing it to be a different size than the device screen.

Making breakpoints with Susy

With Susy you can have as many breakpoints as you need. However, rather than try and remember the various widths for the breakpoints in ems or pixels, let's make a couple of variables, one called $M (for medium-sized viewport widths) and the other called $L for larger ones. We'll add these in the _layouts.scss partial below the other Susy settings:

```
// Breakpoint variables
// ====================================================================
==
$M: 47em; // roughly speaking, around 750px wide with 16px body font
$L: 75em; // roughly speaking, around 1200px wide with 16px body font
```

Remember that our first layout will actually be the absence of media queries: that's our 'accessibility' layout. With these two variables we can therefore ultimately facilitate three layouts, the initial accessibility layout (where no media query is used), a layout at a breakpoint of 47em (around 750px wide assuming a 16px body font) and a layout at a breakpoint of 75em (around 1200px wide with 16px body font).

Susy has a built-in helper mixin called at-breakpoint that we can use to create media queries. Let's see how we can use it alongside the variables we have just defined:

```
nav[role="navigation"] {
  @include at-breakpoint($M) {
    @include span-columns(3,12);
  }
}
.main-content {
  @include at-breakpoint($M) {
    @include prefix(1,12);
    @include span-columns(9 omega,12);
  }
}
```

There are a few things going on here so let's try and take this step by step. First of all, after choosing the relevant selector, an at-breakpoint mixin has been included. Just like any other mixin, it takes an argument. In this case, the argument we are passing to the mixin is the variable we made a moment ago (the one for a medium viewport of 47em in width).

So far, this is effectively saying, "Hey browser, when the viewport is 47em wide I want you to do what's enclosed". In this case, here's what's enclosed in the first rule:

```
nav[role="navigation"] {
  @include at-breakpoint($M) {
    @include span-columns(3,12);
  }
}
```

A new mixin is being used here. It's the span-columns mixin and it's the mixin that tends to be used most frequently when using Susy:

```
@include span-columns(3,12);
```

The span-columns mixin is used to tell Susy how many columns of the grid an element should span. Remember our grid is 12 columns (each currently set to 5em), so in the prior chunk of code, we are spanning three columns on the chapter list and nine on the main content (when the viewport is larger than the size set in our $M variable). We've also used the prefix mixin on the main content to add some space, more information on that shortly. However, notice there is an argument being passed to the span-columns mixin for the main content that isn't in the navigation section. It's the omega argument:

```
@include span-columns(9 omega,12);
```

The omega argument tells Susy that it is the last set of column space in a grid. Knowing this, Susy, by default, floats that element to the opposite direction of the flow (so it will float right for a typical left-to-right layout).

 Susy can also do right-to-left layouts using a couple of direction override settings. Check out http://susy.oddbird.net/ guides/reference/#ref-direction-override for more information.

There's a shorthand for omega that we'll look at shortly.

 It's all Greek to me!

I'm assuming here that you already know that Alpha is the first letter of the Greek alphabet and Omega is the last? Knowing that makes the designation of omega to the final grid items a little more understandable.

If you have used grid systems before, both 'alpha' and 'omega' will probably be familiar concepts. They are used to define an element that is the first or last within a grid. Note however that it isn't necessary to designate anything as Alpha in Susy.

First let's see what our first adventure with Susy has produced. First, the accessibility view. This will apply to any device and also any device with a viewport less than 47 ems wide:

The navigation and main content areas span the full width of smaller viewports (as there is no media query telling them to do otherwise) while the desktop layout we have been working with until now appears as soon as the viewport increases to at least 47em. Here it is:

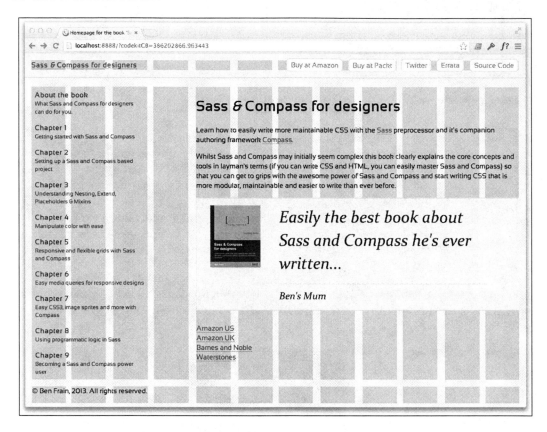

This is the relevant CSS that section of Sass and Compass produces (which comes into play at larger 47em viewports and above):

```
@media (min-width: 47em) {
  [role="navigation"] {
    width: 23.94366%;
    float: left;
    margin-right: 1.40845%;
  }
}


@media (min-width: 47em) {
  .main-content {
    padding-left: 8.4507%;
```

```
    width: 74.64789%;
    float: right;
    margin-right: 0;
  }
}
```

Lovely; Susy has created the media queries based upon the values in the `at-breakpoint` mixin.

Now, let's not kid ourselves, at this point, the visuals and our 'modules' still look like a dog's dinner. However, it is at least visually accessible, regardless of what you view it on.

Furthermore, as we have good semantic markup, tools such as Reader on the iPhone can easily extract the 'main' content. Having pressed **Reader** in Safari on the iPhone, this is the view we get:

It knows what's the navigation and what's the main content and removes the unnecessary content for reading.

Hopefully by this point you are getting a feel of what you can accomplish with Susy, Sass, and Compass.

We now have an 'elastic' Susy-powered grid that works across different viewports and we have authored it with only a few lines of code! Resize the browser window and you will see that the integrity of the grid columns stays intact no matter how small we go, while the grid becomes fixed (centered in the screen) once the viewport size is increased beyond a certain width. Susy, take a bow.

Creating an 'off-canvas' navigation pattern with Susy and jQuery

On the finished site I'll be using an 'off-canvas' technique for showing and hiding the chapter list on smaller viewports. However, as it's a bit of a tangent, although the code is included in the download, I've not detailed how the code works here. Instead, if you'd like to know how it was done, you can head over to http://www.sassandcompass.com/off-canvas-with-susy-and-jquery/.

As it turns out, in this instance, our needs are quite straightforward: a simple 12-column grid. The navigation takes 3 columns and the main content takes 8 (9 if you count the column of padding). Realistically, this is as simple as a layout is likely to get. Thankfully, even when things get more complicated, Susy has a mixin to facilitate your gridular (I know that's not even a word but I'm going with it) needs.

Let's look at some of the features and helpers Susy has.

Removing support for older versions of Internet Explorer

Susy has code built in to deal with inconsistencies in Internet Explorer 6 and 7. If you know you won't be supporting older versions of IE in your project, you can remove support by adding and amending these Compass variables:

```
$legacy-support-for-ie   : false;
$legacy-support-for-ie6  : $legacy-support-for-ie;
$legacy-support-for-ie7  : $legacy-support-for-ie;
```

Just to be crystal clear, you only need to include and amend these variables if you wish to remove support for older versions of Internet Explorer. In this instance, we are including these variables to remove support for both IE6 and IE7 (the last two variables are set to be equal to the first, which is in turn set to be false).

Removing support for older versions of IE is a micro-optimization in this instance and is only useful if you are certain you have no need to support those browsers.

Creating an entirely fluid grid

While Susy creates an elastic grid (that flexes to a point and then become fixed) by default, it can easily convert a grid to be fully fluid (in which it completely and proportionally fills all the available space). This can be achieved by adding this variable below the existing grid settings:

```
$container-style: fluid;
```

And here is how that looks in the browser:

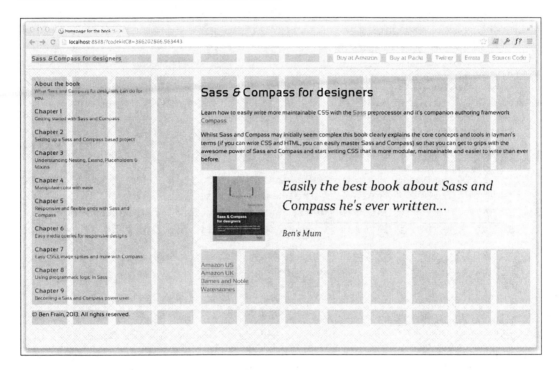

Be aware you can also set a percentage width for a fluid grid container with the following variable:

```
$container-width: 80%;
```

Creating a static 'fixed' grid

Susy is of most help when creating elastic grids( ) (that flex to a point and then become fixed) and fluid grids (that fluidly fill the entire size of the viewport).

However, there may be instances when you are handed a graphics composite with the remit of creating a fixed version of the grid system in use (http://960.gs, for example).

If you need a static grid system, you can do this easily with Susy; just add a single variable (be aware that you will need to edit, remove, or comment out any existing $container-style variable):

```
$container-style: static;
```

If you use that and resize the viewport (make the browser window smaller), you will see that the grid remains entirely static until it hits a relevant breakpoint.

Using Susy grid helpers

Let's revert to the elastic grid now and comment out those prior variables. Remember that Sass will remove comments on compile so if you would like to leave them in place (for reference), don't feel bad about it. For clarification, here is the relative section of the _layout.scss partial that defines the grid:

```
// Grid layout variables (http://susy.oddbird.net/)
// ====================================================================
==
@import "susy";
$total-columns    : 12;              // a 12-column grid
$column-width     : 5em;             // each column is 5em wide
$gutter-width     : 1em;             // 1em gutters between columns
$grid-padding     : $gutter-width;   // grid-padding equal to gutters
$border-box-sizing: true;
```

As mentioned, Susy has a few grid helper mixins to solve common layout issues.

Prefix, Suffix, and Pad

prefix, suffix, and pad are all mixins that make adding padding before or after (or both before and after) columns simple.

Prefix

We've already used the `prefix` mixin to add a column of space before the main content:

```
.main-content {
  @include prefix(1,12);
  @include span-columns(9 omega,12);
}
```

We can already see that column of padding in the browser between the navigation and main content:

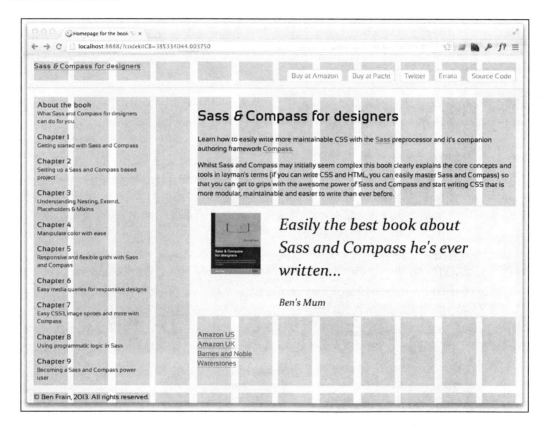

As with the `span-columns` mixin, pass the number of columns that need to prefix the item and then the context (12 in this case as we have a 12-column grid).

> If not using the `border-box` box-sizing model, be aware that you'd need to amend the `span-columns` mixin too. For example, in the example before, if adding a prefix of 1, you would need to adjust the `span-columns` mixin to 8.

Suffix

We could achieve a similar effect by using the `suffix` helper mixin instead. Let's use `suffix` on the navigation instead and remove the `prefix` mixin from the main-content:

```
nav[role="navigation"] {
  @include span-columns(3, 12);
  @include suffix(1,12);
}
.main-content {
  @include span-columns(9 omega, 12);
}
```

Here is what that gives us in the browser:

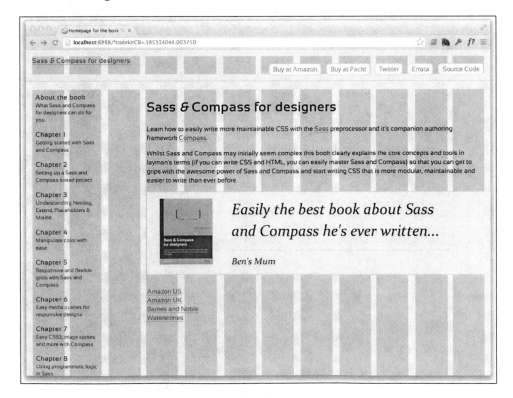

Notice that because the padding from the `suffix` helper has been applied to the navigation area, it has decreased the amount of available space for the navigation.

Pad

We can split the difference and apply some padding to both sides of an element in one go. For example:

```
nav[role="navigation"] {
  @include span-columns(3, 12);
}
.main-content {
  @include span-columns(9 omega, 12);
  @include pad(1,1,12);
}
```

Here is what that gives us in the browser:

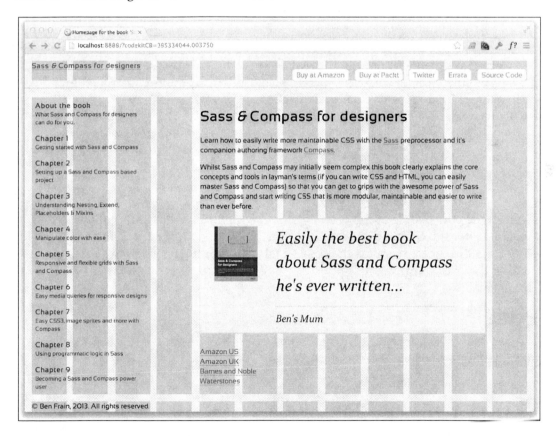

The pad helper deals with both left and right padding in one go. The syntax is as follows: number of columns of padding on the left, number of columns of padding on the right, and then context. To exemplify, if there needed to be two columns of padding on the right and one on the left, you would alter the mixin to this:

```
@include pad(1,2,12);
```

Pre, Post, Squish, Push, and Pull

Just like the padding helpers, Susy has helper mixins to more easily administer margins within a grid. They work in a very similar manner. The helpers are called pre, post, squish, push, and pull.

Pre

The pre mixin applies margin before an element. For example, to add a column's worth of margin before an element, you would add this mixin:

```
@include pre(1);
```

Be aware that if you add margin to an element with pre, you may need to adjust the amount of columns with the span-columns mixin. Therefore, to adjust the main content to give the same visual effect with pre instead of prefix or pad, we could write this:

```
.main-content {
  @include pre(1);
  @include span-columns(8 omega, 12);
}
```

To clarify for the people at the back not paying attention, there are 9 columns available after the chapters section; we want 1 to be used for margin and the other 8 for the content (and as the content takes up the final column we're passing the omega argument).

Post

The post mixin does what you would expect, it's the opposite of pre, adding margin after an element. For example:

```
@include post(3);
```

Would add three columns of margin after the element.

Squish

The `squish` mixin is the margin equivalent of `pad`. It allows margins to be added both before and after an element. As with `pad`, the first argument is for passing in the number of columns of space needed on the left and the second is for the space on the right. As an example, if we wanted to add a 2-columns margin on either side of an element we would write this:

```
@include squish(2,2,12);
```

 Keep in mind, however, that if you are adding the `squish` mixin to an element that already has `omega`, then things will look screwy (that's a technical term by the way). That's because the `omega` argument already removes the margin on one side.

Push and Pull

Push works exactly like `pre`, so both those mixins can be used interchangeably. Pull on the other hand is slightly different. It adds negative margin before an element. Again, it accepts the same arguments you are now used to with these Susy grid helpers, namely, `columns`, `context` and `from`. Here is an example of the syntax, where we want a single column of negative margin on an element:

```
@include pull(1);
```

 Again, be aware that if you are using this on an element that is already floated right with the `omega` argument, it will have no effect.

Grids within grids

As already mentioned, Susy makes it easy to create grids within grids. Let's use this feature to space out the section of links beneath the block quote (the links to Amazon and Barnes and Noble bookstores).

We'll separate the styles that will affect this area across two partials. We only want the `_layout.scss` partial to contain structural layout so we can add the Susy-related rules there:

```scss
// Grid override for purchase links
 @include with-grid-settings(4,12em,1.5em,0) {
   .purchase-links-wrapper {
     @include container;
   }
   .purchase-link {
     @include span-columns(1);
     @include nth-omega(4n);
   }
};
```

There are a few things going on here, so let's break that chunk of code down. First of all, we are including the `with-grid-settings` mixin:

```scss
@include with-grid-settings(4,8em,1.5em,0) {
```

This lets us create a new grid, with different settings, within an existing grid. The syntax of the `with-grid-settings` mixin is: number of columns (4 columns in the preceding example), the width of each column (`8em` each in our example), the gutter width between each column (`1.5em` in our example), and finally any padding for the outside of the grid (there's zero padding for our example).

Any rules that need the new grid applied are then nested within. We will set the `.purchase-links-wrapper` selector for the unordered list (`<ul class="purchase-links-wrapper">`) as the container for the grid:

```scss
@include with-grid-settings(4,8em,1.5em,0) {
   .purchase-links-wrapper {
     @include container;
   }
```

Then, we set each link item to span a column each (it's a four-column grid and there are four links) and crucially, we are using the Susy `nth-omega` mixin. Let me explain what that does.

nth-omega mixin

The Susy `nth-omega` mixin is a shortcut for setting margins on the last (`omega`) item. As there are four items, we are telling Susy that the fourth of them is the final one and should have the relevant `omega` styles applied:

```
@include with-grid-settings(4,12em,1.5em,0) {
  .purchase-links-wrapper {
    @include container;
  }
  .purchase-link {
    @include span-columns(1);
    @include nth-omega(4n);
  }
};
```

What the nth?

If you're not familiar with nth-child selectors, here's what you need to know. When it comes to selecting elements in the tree structure of the DOM (Document Object Model, or more simplistically, the elements in a page's markup) CSS Level 3 selectors give us incredible flexibility with a few nth-based rules, : nth-child(n), :nth-last-child(n), :nth-of-type(n), and :nth-last-of- type(n). The (n) parameter can be used in a couple of ways:

- **Used as an integer**: For example, :nth-child(2) would select the second item.
- **Used as a numeric expression**: For example, :nth-child(3n+1) would start at 1 and then select every third element.
- Want to try out different nth-based selectors? Check out Lea Verou's online tool at http://lea.verou.me/demos/nth.html.

The nth-omega mixin actually defaults to last so we can actually just write @include nth-omega; in this instance and it will work just as well.

While working on the links, let's remove the background gradient from the main grids and add it to the nested grid. Here's the complete section:

```
// Grid override for purchase links
@include with-grid-settings(4,12em,1.5em,0) {
  .purchase-links-wrapper {
    @include container;
    @include susy-grid-background;
  }
  .purchase-link {
    @include span-columns(1);
    @include nth-omega;
  }
};
```

With that code in place, this is what we get in the browser:

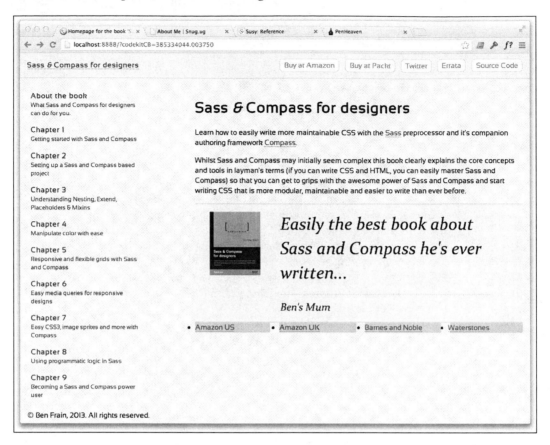

Now for the module itself (we're adding these styles into the `_modules.scss` partial):

```
.purchase-links-wrapper {
  list-style: none;
  margin: 30px 0 0 0;
}
```

And for now, that's it. I have something planned for these links, which we'll get to in *Chapter 7, Easy CSS3, Image Sprites, and More with Compass*. Until then, we've got the grid within a grid taking care of the layout of these links:

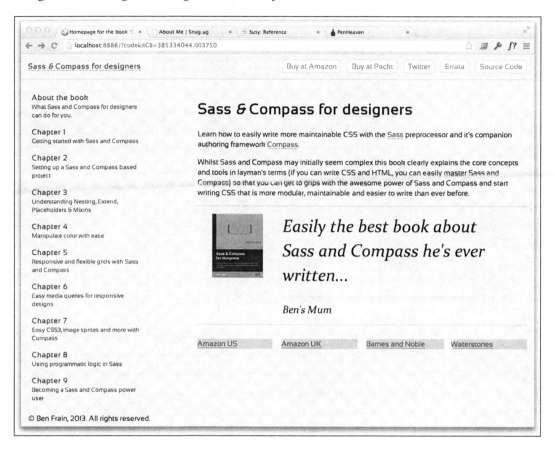

Sub-pixel rounding issues

I have a confession; I've been keeping something from you. Take a look at the following screenshot and if you are the kind of designer that freaks out when there is a pixel astray, please make sure you're sitting down.

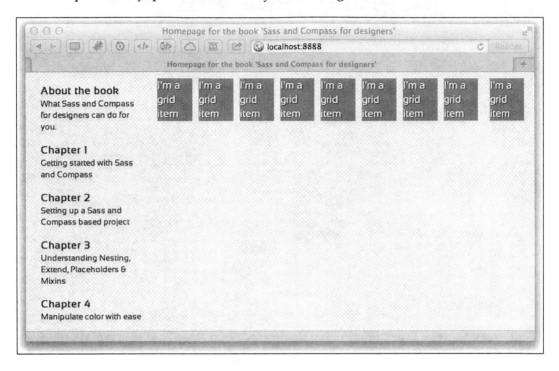

Can you see an odd-sized gap before the final red grid item? The screenshot is taken in Safari 6. This same problem isn't apparent in Chrome or Firefox. That's because Safari rounds down sub-pixels. Why?

Although the outer dimensions of the grid (the context) may be set as ems, all the column widths within the grid are defined as percentages. That's a large part of what enables the grid to be responsive to different viewports.

To actually paint the page, browsers convert percentage values into pixels. Parts of pixels cannot be rendered so they are rounded. The problem is that some browsers round up, some don't, and some do something else. Most of the time this isn't an issue. In some browsers, in some instances it is, typically when there are multiple grid items one after the other. What do we do about this? First we need to understand a little about why these tiny sub-pixel discrepancies become so noticeable.

Why sub-pixel rounding errors occur

As we now know, ordinarily, Susy works by floating grid items one after the other. The position of each item in the grid is relevant to the item that preceded it. With multiple grid items, the space between each is a point where a rounding 'error' could occur. The more elements, the more accumulated discrepancy. As the grid elements are all floated left and any omega column(s) are floated in the opposite direction, all the rounding errors are effectively visible in the gap before the omega columns.

John Albin Wilkins was the first person I know to document the sub-pixel rounding issue in detail here: `http://palantir.net/ blog/responsive-design-s-dirty-little-secret`. His own grid system, called Zen (`http://zengrids.com`), uses 'container relative' positioning to minimize the issue. We'll look at container relative positioning shortly.

I also had my own little grumble about sub-pixel rounding here: `http://benfra.in/1z3`. Since then, Susy has added its own method for dealing with the issue — also detailed in the next section.

Container relative positioning

While items in a Susy grid are typically laid out relative to the items that preceded them, there is a method called **container relative positioning** popularized by the Zen grid system (more details on Zen in the previous information box). With container relative positioning, the items are spaced relative to the inside edge of the containing element. This negates much of the pixel rounding issues because you're only suffering a single rounding error (the distance from the inside edge of the container to the element) rather than multiples all culminating in a potential glaring visual disparity like the one we saw earlier.

However, the method is not without drawbacks. To explain, let's reconsider how Susy usually does things.

Standard Susy syntax and output

In the previous grid, with nine grid items, it's possible to write this:

```
.grid-item {
  @include span-columns(1,12);
    @include nth-omega;
}
```

And here's the relevant CSS produced that takes care of all nine items:

```
.grid-item {
  width: 7.04225%;
  float: left;
  margin-right: 1.40845%;
}
.grid-item:last-child {
  float: right;
  margin-right: 0;
}
```

Nice and compact output. However, the code needed to lay grid elements out using the container relative method is, by necessity, more verbose.

Unlike traditional floats, with container-relative positioning, it's necessary to specify the position of each individual item in the grid. Susy makes authoring these rules fairly trivial with the `isolate-grid` mixin.

The isolate-grid mixin

To illustrate how the `isolate-grid` mixin can fix our problem, first of all, in the markup, we'll need a wrapping `div` around those grid items (I've given it an HTML class of `grid-item-wrapper`). This will position that block of grid items in the normal span-columns manner. Then for each `grid-item` we will use the `isolate-grid` mixin to position the interior grid items with container-relative positioning:

```
[role="navigation"] {
  @include span-columns(3, 12);
}
.grid-item-wrapper {
  @include span-columns(9 omega,12);
}
.grid-item {
  @include isolate-grid(1,9);
}
```

By wrapping the grid items, it also allows us to set the context for the nine grid items. The arguments being passed to the `isolate-grid` mixin are the number of columns each item should span (1 in our example) and the context (the number of available columns) available. Here is the result in Safari:

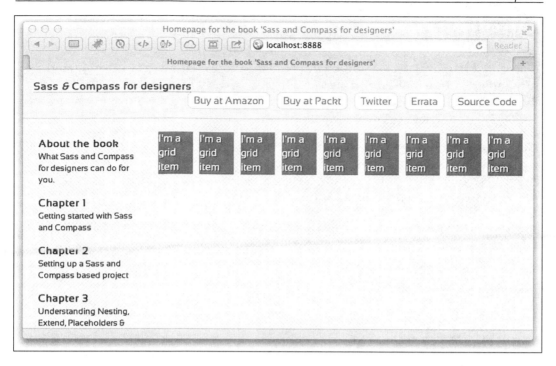

I think you'll agree that's much better visually. However, there is a price to pay. This isolation method, by necessity, produces more verbose CSS. As the items aren't floated one after the other, (margin and negative margin is used on either side to position the items), each item in the isolated grid needs selecting and positioning individually. Take a look at the generated CSS and you'll see a number of `nth-child` based rules, each selecting and positioning each item in the grid.

Susy also has an `isolate` mixin that works alongside the standard `span-columns` mixin to try and address discrepancies with particular grid elements. However, it's less effective if there are multiple grid elements. If you think it could be just the medicine you need, head over to `http://susy.oddbird.net/guides/reference/#ref-isolate` for more information.

Be aware, therefore, that while the authoring experience for the isolation method is easy enough, it does produce more CSS code. However, if the situation requires it, a few extra lines of CSS code is a small price to pay for a neater grid.

Summary

We've covered a lot in this chapter. We have installed the Susy grid system, included it in our project, and then implemented it to create a grid-based layout that responds to different viewport sizes. If we were always using Susy, we could use the `at-breakpoint` mixin to create media queries, changing the layout structure or appearance of certain elements when needed.

However, there will likely be situations when a grid system isn't needed. Therefore, we need some independent way of easily creating responsive styles. In the next chapter, we will learn how to create our own media query mixin, giving us the power to easily change styles for any element inline.

In today's responsive design world, it is one of the Sass and Compass features I find most compelling.

Advanced Media Queries with Sass and Mixins

6

With the plethora of devices that now access the Internet, it makes sense to build web properties responsively.

Unless you have been living on a private island for the last few years (if you have, don't bother watching the end of *Lost*; it is not worth it) you will know the core ingredients of a responsive design are a fluid layout, fluid media, and media queries.

We looked at fluid grids extensively in the last chapter and learned how the Compass plugin, Susy, can make short work of even the most complicated layouts. While Susy also has built-in support for changing the design at arbitrary breakpoints, there may be occasions when you want to target styles based on media queries and don't need Susy elsewhere in the project.

 When talking about media queries in relation to responsive designs, we usually mean minimum or maximum widths. Furthermore, the term **breakpoint** is literally the point at which a design breaks when you change the browser's window dimensions; becoming ugly, hard to read, or just plain glitchy. It's at the breakpoint where you create a new media query to fix it.

In this chapter, therefore, we will:

- Create a custom mixin to create media queries
- Create a number of 'breakpoints' set as variables
- Use our custom mixin to place media query based rules throughout our styles
- Understand how Sass media query bubbling works
- Explore the impact that random media queries have on our compiled CSS

Media queries in Sass

Before we get into fun and games, it makes sense to understand where Sass can help us with media queries. Media queries can be used for all manner of things: viewport width, viewport height, device width, device height, orientation, viewport aspect ratio, device-aspect ratio, color, color index, monochrome, resolution, scan, and grid. In this instance, I'm concentrating on viewport width, as that's primarily what we use when styling responsive websites.

 Want to read the W3C specification for media queries? You can find it at http://www.w3.org/TR/css3-mediaqueries/.

When I started building sites responsively, I was using plain CSS. All the 'normal' styles would be written first and then the media queries would be written at the end of the file. Here is a very simplified example of what I mean:

```css
.style {
  width: 100%;
}

/* All the 'normal' styles...

...

*/
/* First breakpoint */
@media only screen and (min-width: 320px) {
  .styles {
    width: 80%;
  }
}
/* Second breakpoint */
@media only screen and (min-width: 480px) {
  .styles {
    width: 70%;
  }
}
/* Third breakpoint */
@media only screen and (min-width: 600px) {
  .styles {
    width: 60%;
  }
}
```

Admittedly, in this example, that doesn't seem like such a burden, but once hundreds of styles are defined it can be troublesome separating them out at the end of the file into the various media queries needed. There is often a lot of style duplication across all the media queries just to get the desired effect.

In short, it is frustrating work at best and has been known to force expletives from even the mildest mannered of web developers.

Using a media query partial to separate media query based styles

It's possible to go on defining media query styles at the end of style sheets. There is nothing wrong with that practice. Even using that methodology, with Sass, the organization of those styles can be made a little easier by separating all the media query-based styles into a partial file called something suitable (such as _media-queries.scss) and then importing it at the end of the main styles in the manner you are now accustomed to:

```
@import "partials/media-queries";
```

Inline media queries with Sass

However, while we can split media queries into a separate partial, hopefully, in this chapter, you'll be convinced there is a better way of authoring media queries with Sass.

Let's suppose a container needs to be different widths at different viewports. With Sass, we can produce exactly the same outcome as our prior example by writing the following code:

```scss
.style {
  color: $color1;
  @include MQ(Splus) {
    width: 80%;
  }
  @include MQ(Mplus) {
    width: 70%;
  }
  @include MQ(Lplus) {
    width: 60%;
  }
}
```

After choosing a selector, any property and value pairs that will be identical across various viewport sizes (color and font-family perhaps) are declared.

Then, the various media query breakpoint styles are nested within. These nested media queries 'bubble up' and produce the same CSS as before:

```css
.style {
  color: red;
}
@media only screen and (min-width: 30em) {
  .style {
    width: 80%;
  }
}
@media only screen and (min-width: 47em) {
  .style {
    width: 70%;
  }
}
@media only screen and (min-width: 75em) {
  .style {
    width: 60%;
  }
}
```

Writing media queries this way may not immediately seem like a big win but the larger the project, the more preferential it becomes to declare styles for different viewports inline with any existing styles. The principal benefit of this approach is that you can contain the various visual permutations of an element in a single block of code, regardless of the viewport it is displayed in.

That is a huge win so you may be wondering what the rub is. The only downside is that it produces as many separate media queries as you declare in the Sass. Now, that may or may not concern you. If you are reading this in horror and wondering why on earth I would advocate littering CSS with potentially hundreds of media query rules, I'll address those concerns shortly! For now, let's just see how we can facilitate writing media queries inline with Sass in this manner.

For things like media query mixins, consider creating a snippet in your text editor or a tool like **TextExpander** so that just writing an abbreviation creates the text. This makes it virtually effortless to create a media query when you need it. Why do a job that a machine can easily do for you? For example, I have mine set so that when I type mmq it creates:

```
@include MQ(XL) {


}
```

And when I type ,comscsssub or ,comscssmain it creates the comment blocks I use throughout my Sass files to divide sections of code. It also comes in handy for certain syntaxes I can never remember, such as CSS3 background gradients. Sky's the limit!

Creating a mixin to easily handle media queries

Before we can write media queries with a Sass mixin, we need to actually create the mixin that will generate the media query code. The mixin we'll write is based upon one created by Compass creator and Sass core team member Chris Eppstein, which he posted at https://gist.github.com/1215856#file_6_media_queries.scss.

Defining breakpoints as variables

A further advantage of writing media queries this way with Sass is that we can define variables for the breakpoints in the design. Then each media query relates to those breakpoints.

As the breakpoints are set as variables, they can be easily amended. It is then a trivial job if breakpoint values need to be changed throughout. Just amend the variable value and everything else just falls into place.

It is also easy to switch the units being used for the breakpoints. Want to switch from pixel-based variable values to em-based? Piece of cake, edit the breakpoint values and the media queries are now em based. It is like magic, trust me!

OK, less talk, more action. Let's get started defining the variables and making the mixin.

Here is what we'll go with for the variables:

```
// Breakpoint variables
// =======================================================================
==
$XS: 18em; // roughly speaking, around 288px wide with 16px body font
$S: 30em; // roughly speaking, around 480px wide with 16px body font
$M: 43em; // roughly speaking, around 688px wide with 16px body font
$L: 57em; // roughly speaking, around 912px wide with 16px body font
```

You can add those in to the _variables.scss partial, or if you would rather, add them to the _mixins.scss file as that is where we will be adding the next block of code, the MQ mixin itself. Also remember that these values are not (and should not) be set in stone—they are whatever suits your design. Here is the mixin itself:

```
@mixin MQ($canvas) {
  @if $canvas == XS {
    @media only screen and (min-width: $XS) and (max-width: $S - 1) {
@content; }
  }
  @else if $canvas == S {
    @media only screen and (min-width: $S) and (max-width: $M - 1) { @
content; }
  }
  @else if $canvas == M {
    @media only screen and (min-width: $M) and (max-width: $L - 1) { @
content; }
  }
  @else if $canvas == L {
    @media only screen and (min-width: $L) and (max-width: $XL - 1) {
@content; }
  }
  @else if $canvas == XL {
    @media only screen and (min-width: $XL) and (max-width: $XXL - 1)
{ @content; }
  }
}
```

I know that probably looks like complete gibberish but there are two reasons it should not bother you:

- Firstly, it's not necessary to understand any of that mixin. It can just be pasted into a Sass file and then used in the manner we'll cover shortly.

- Secondly, like all the mixins we are using, we can break it down and understand what exactly it is doing. After doing that, you will see it's really just the code equivalent of a pussycat (and not the scary lion you perhaps first thought).

Here comes the science…

How the MQ media query mixin works

Let's get a handle on how this mixin works by looking at it bit by bit:

```
@mixin MQ($canvas) {
   @if $canvas == XS {
```

First we use the `@mixin` directive and name the mixin (I've called mine `MQ` for media query as it's terse but you can call yours whatever you like). Then we open the parenthesis and pass in the argument. In this instance it's a variable called `$canvas`. Then we close the parenthesis and open the first curly brace.

Now comes an `@if` control directive. That perhaps sounds like something a smug neck-bearded nerd might say but all one needs to grasp is that we are heading into a series of `if` statements.

If you have any exposure to programming, `if/else` statements will be second nature. For everyone else, here is what you need to know: `if/else` statements are just like ordering from a bar. "If you have Southern Comfort, I'll have that, otherwise I'll have Jim Beam". It's the same deal here; if this is true, do this, or if this is true do something else. See? Easy.

So with that incredibly technical explanation in our minds, here is our first `if` statement:

```
@if $canvas == XS {
```

It is simply saying; if the value passed to the mixin (the canvas size) is equal to `XS` (the double equal signs means 'equal to'), then do the thing in the curly braces. In this case, the part within the curly braces is this:

```
@media only screen and (min-width: $XS) and (max-width: $S - 1) { @
content; }
```

Hopefully this is a little more straightforward. It's a normal media query `min-width` to `max-width` syntax with the only exception being that the `$XS` variable is placed as the `min-width` value and the `$S` value is passed to the `max-width` value with a tiny bit of math; a minus 1 after it. This is so that the range we want the media query to apply to goes up to but doesn't include the value of `$S` (as the next media query will start there).

You will notice that there is a `@content` section inside the media query. This just tells Sass where the actual rules that will be enclosed by the media query will reside.

All the subsequent sections that begin `@else if` are just variations on the same theme. We can also copy and amend those existing statements to create rules that will cater for any possible eventuality. Let's give that a whirl.

Variations on a theme

At present, our mixin has us covered if we want to target styles for certain width ranges, for example, between the S and M ranges (remember, we are setting those values in the _variables.scss file). However, often it makes more sense to target rules based upon any viewport width above a certain range. To exemplify, instead of this:

```
@media only screen and (min-width: 30em) and (max-width: 46em) {

}
```

Where we are limiting the styles to a range between the minimum and maximum values, we want to produce something like this:

```
@media only screen and (min-width: 30em) {

}
```

So, let's add to our mixin to include this functionality. Below the existing @else if statements (right before the final closing curly brace), add this:

```
@else if $canvas == XSplus {
  @media only screen and (min-width: $XS) { @content; }
}
```

With that in place, we can pass a new argument to our mixin when we need it. For example:

```
@include MQ(XSplus) {

  /* styles here */

}
```

This produces the following CSS:

```
@media only screen and (min-width: 18em) {
    /* styles here */
}
```

It's a really flexible system. Want to create an @else if statement for a range between S and L? Easy peasy…

```
@else if $canvas == StoL {
  @media only screen and (min-width: $S) and (max-width: $L - 1) { @
content; }
}
```

I'm going to add a few more `@else if` statements into the mixin which you can find in the code download (remember, you can get it all at `http://sassandcompass.com`). Hopefully, with the ones we have covered and the additional ones in the code it should make sense and give you the confidence to amend the mixin for your own usage.

Well done, you've just got your head around a fairly powerful mixin.

I don't know about you but I'm itching to put this to use now so let's crack open the `index.html` page and our `_modules.scss` file and see what fun we can have with it.

Writing inline media queries

First off, be aware that there have been a few more unrelated amendments to the HTML (and some more styles added in the Sass purely for presentational purposes). As we're not going to be writing any styles to target old IE, the conditional comments that provide helper classes for it have been removed.

Now we just have the following code at the start of the `index.html` file:

```
<!doctype html>
<html class="no-js" lang="en">
<head>
```

With that little bit of housekeeping out of the way, the markup for the main `headline` area has changed a little:

```
<h1 class="headline">
  <span class="headline-hero">Sass</span>
  <i class="ampersand">&amp;</i>
  <span class="headline-sidekick">Compass</span>
  <span class="forwho">for designers</span>
</h1>
```

With that markup in mind, here's the first block of style I'm adding to the `_modules.scss` file:

```
.headline {
  @extend %clearfix;
  margin: 0;
  font-weight: 400;
  line-height: 4.1em;
  @include MQ(XSplus) {
    font-size: 1.76em;
  }
}
```

```
@include MQ(Splus) {
    font-size: 2.5em;
}
@include MQ(Mplus) {
    font-size: 2.8em;
}
@include MQ(Lplus) {
    font-size: 3.7em;
}
}
```

Our new mixin has been used four times on this one class alone: once for viewports above XS (XSplus), once for viewports above S (Splus), again for viewports wider than M (Mplus), and finally for viewports wider than L (Lplus). All that's being changed is the font size for the different viewport ranges.

We'll look at what that gives us in the browser in a moment but for now, it's perhaps worth noting that for this chapter, more placeholder styles have been saved in _placeholders.scss. A couple more fonts have also been added, courtesy of http://fontsquirrel.com. They're referenced in the _fonts.scss partial (and implemented with the same syntax that we used in *Chapter 3, Nesting, Extend, Placeholders, and Mixins*).

> From a maintainability point of view, whenever utility styles are needed in a project it may be worth extending them (using @extend) from a placeholder style. So, for example, font declaration, clearfixes, default transitions, and the like—they are all prime candidates for placeholder selectors. As the placeholders are referenced multiple times in a project, it will ultimately become one large combination selector to address that single CSS function. By using the _placeholder.scss partial in this way it's possible to build up a large placeholder file that can be carried from project to project and only the styles that are extended (using @extend) get written out to CSS. You don't have to follow suit but that's the way I roll.

Without further ado, let's see what we have in the browser now at various viewport widths. The following screenshot shows the page displayed in a 1140 px wide viewport:

The following screenshot is a 700px wide viewport:

And the following image shows what that area looks like on an iPhone (320 px viewport):

You can see how the media queries have controlled the size of the headline area at various viewports. The following is the CSS that the `.headline` style has generated:

```css
.headline {
  font-weight: 400;
  line-height: 4.1em;
}
@media only screen and (min-width: 18em) {
  .headline {
    font-size: 1.76em;
  }
}
@media only screen and (min-width: 30em) {
  .headline {
    font-size: 2.5em;
  }
}
@media only screen and (min-width: 43em) {
```

```
    .headline {
      font-size: 2.8em;
    }
  }
  @media only screen and (min-width: 57em) {
    .headline {
      font-size: 3.7em;
    }
  }
```

Let's look at another example. Let's add a little padding around the main content area at smaller viewports and alter the font size there too:

```
// Text in the main content area
// ============================================================
.main-content {
  @include MQ(Sneg) {
    padding: 0 1em;
  }
  p {
    line-height: 1.7em;
    @include MQ(Sneg) {
      font-size: 1.1em;
    }
  }
}
```

You will notice that these two media queries are nested at different levels. How does this *bubble up* in the generated CSS?

```
@media only screen and (max-width: 30em) {
  .main-content {
    padding: 0 1em;
  }
}
.main-content p {
  line-height: 1.7em;
}
@media only screen and (max-width: 30em) {
  .main-content p {
    font-size: 1.1em;
  }
}
```

As they both had the same argument passed to the mixin, they have both generated identical media queries around their respective selectors.

Now, as alluded to earlier, if this technique is employed throughout the styles of an entire website, it is going to result in many repeated media query statements in the compiled CSS. Every time the MQ mixin is used, it is going to generate another. Is that a problem? As ever in web design, it depends. Generally, to help me decide whether these replicated media queries will be a problem I start with the following question. Will a human or a system need to read the generated CSS?

Let me expand on that. Generating media queries inline may not be the best choice if the generated CSS is to be taken and used by another developer (it will need to be decided between yourself and the other developer(s)). However, if the CSS will be uploaded direct to a server, I rarely give it a second thought. Here is why.

Gzip and CSS compression = victory!

First off, let's revisit something we have touched upon already: `http://httparchive.org/interesting.php#bytesperpage`

That link shows that as far as web assets go, CSS is almost always the smallest in terms of file size. Therefore, CSS file size optimization, in general, is a micro-optimization. That does not mean we should abandon the pursuit of economical CSS but we should be aware that optimizing a single image on the same page would probably save more in terms of file size.

Secondly, the web server that will be serving the CSS will be (or certainly should be) using gzip. This will automatically compress the files *over the wire* for us, shrinking them to a fraction of their original size.

Gzip is the format that web servers and browsers use to zip and unzip files. When we need to compress something so it takes up less space, making it easier to transfer down the wire (typically email attachments, backup files, and the like), we zip it up. When we receive a zip file we open it and the enclosed contents expand out. That is essentially what gzip facilitates between the server and the browser.

The server asks the browser if it accepts gzip files and if it does, that is how it sends the assets it can zip up. It's a way of ensuring that data is sent and received as quickly as possible. If you want to test whether your own websites are using gzip, head over to `http://gzipwtf.com` and enter their URLs.

If gzip compresses files on the server, do we even need to bother compressing our CSS before upload? In short, yes, my young Padawan. And here's why.

Minification/compression (the part Sass does when we specify a compressed output in the Compass `config.rb` file) removes comments and whitespace. If this was not removed before gzip got to it, that information would have to be retained so that the file could be expanded (whitespace, comments, and all) on receipt. However, let's look at a tangible example of all these optimization shenanigans and see if we can draw any conclusions.

Testing the real-world difference between inline and grouped media queries

As I'm arguing that the difference between media queries grouped together and those written inline is so negligible as to be irrelevant, I'd better back that up with a little empirical evidence.

To illustrate the point, indulge me in a simple test. By the end of this chapter, there are 20 media queries defined inline for the `http://sassandcompass.com` site we are building.

First of all, uncompressed, the file size of the CSS itself is 14.1 KB (14,145 bytes).

If that uncompressed CSS file is gzipped, the file size comes down to 3 KB (3,058 bytes).

Let's back up and compress that CSS with Sass (using the `output_style = :compressed` option in the `config.rb` file). At this point, the file size comes down to 11.8 KB (11,805 bytes). This is as opposed to 14.1 KB/14,145 bytes uncompressed.

If the compressed CSS file is then gzipped, the size still only comes down to 2.7 KB (2,785 bytes). This is a slight improvement over the 3KB/3,058 bytes when not compressed first).

So, before even worrying about media queries, this tells us that both compressing and gzipping the CSS are worth doing. The smallest likely size this CSS file will travel over the wire from server to user would be around 2.7 KB—that's tiny!

I don't know about you but I'd be interested to know what difference it would make if all the media queries were combined instead—so every style relevant to a particular breakpoint was contained within a single breakpoint at the end of the CSS.

Such is my commitment to research and furthering the human race's understanding of CSS I undertook this monumental task (only took about 30 minutes so hold the knighthood). The resultant CSS file is saved in the CSS folder and called `combined-mq-test.css`. The following are the results:

Uncompressed, the file size of the CSS is 13.4 KB (13,461 bytes). That is already a slight improvement on our inline version.

If that uncompressed CSS file is gzipped, the file size comes down to 3 KB (3,012 bytes). At this point, again, it is a slight improvement over the 3KB/3058 bytes of the inline version.

If that CSS was compressed first, the file size is 11.1 KB (11,135 bytes). This file is saved as `combined-mq-test_compressed.css`. Our inline file version was 11.8 KB/11,805 bytes at this point.

If the compressed CSS file is gzipped, the size comes down to 2.7 KB (2,755 bytes). This is compared to a 2.7 KB/2,785 bytes size file for the inline version of the media queries.

The conclusion? The difference over the wire between the smallest version of each CSS (inline media queries and combined) is just 35 bytes! A difference of just over 1 percent. To put that into perspective, the image of the book on the home page is 33.6 KB/33,669 bytes. That one image is over twice the size of the uncompressed CSS!

Granted, this is but a single site and we have not finished our style sheet yet but the results compound the results I have found every time I have performed the test on a style sheet. For almost every conceivable situation, the difference in file size between the inline and combined versions of media queries is so negligible it is simply not worth spending time worrying about. I favor ease of authorship and maintainability of code over micro-optimizations of this type almost every time.

It could be argued that on large style sheets, CSS optimizations such as this are important and should be addressed. However, from my own experience, on larger scale sites (where views per day are measured in the thousands and millions) I would still spend my *performance-focused* time elsewhere first. Even if just concerning ourselves with CSS, concentrating on property performance (which affects the speed a browser can 'draw' the page) would get my time before CSS file size optimization any day!

Hopefully, if you had any concerns about this aspect of using media queries inline, this little exercise has put your mind at ease. However, at this point, whilst we are checking our output, it is time to dive a little deeper and review what we have done so far.

Reviewing CSS code

Although when authoring styles in Sass it's probable you will spend less time looking at the resultant CSS, that does not mean you shouldn't review the CSS periodically. Why is this necessary?

For me, principally, it is because with the nesting capability of Sass, sometimes the depth of the generated CSS selector is not obvious from a cursory glance at the Sass file. To exemplify this, currently here is the block of code for the list of chapter summaries that run down the left side on larger viewports:

```
.chapter-summary {
  a {
    @extend %block;
    padding: .5em;
    color: $color10;
    opacity: .8;
    border: none;
    &:hover {
      opacity: 1;
    }
    &:visited {
      opacity: .9;
    }
    b {
      @extend %block;
    }
    span {
      @extend %block;
      font-size: .8em;
    }
  }
}
```

Now, that does not look so bad, but with those `@extends` in place, here is the CSS:

```
.chapter-summary a, .chapter-summary a b, .chapter-summary a span,
.off-canvas-navigation, .sidebar-button, .headline-sidekick {
  display: block;
}
```

My main problem with the selectors here is that in some instances, they are more specific than they need to be. For example, instead of this:

```
.chapter-summary a span {}
```

I could just have the following code:

```
.chapter-summary span {}
```

That way, a span can be used elsewhere within the chapter-summary class without needing to nest it within an anchor link. Perhaps better still, an HTML class could just be added to the span itself.

Let's look at the Sass written thus far and *un-nest* any styles possible. To spot these at a glance perhaps skim up and down the CSS and look for any lines that seem overly long. They are usually ones where selectors are too many levels deep and could possibly be refactored.

While we want related styles to be as modular and portable as possible, perhaps we can achieve the same effect by grouping and commenting the associated and related styles and have the additional benefit of less specific selectors.

I would encourage you to take a good look at the CSS that you are generating periodically to catch things like this and mend your wicked ways (I consider myself a work in progress). It will save your time and other developers' time tracking down specificity issues in the future.

Depending upon what you are building, it is worth remembering that browsers read CSS right to left, so the right-most selector is the most important. It could be argued that we could help the browser paint the styles faster still by adding an additional class to the a, span, and b tags and reference those in our CSS. For example:

```
.chapter-summary-link {}
.chapter-summary-span {}
.chapter-summary-b {}
```

I've also used the universal selector * at times in my styles which many would say is about as vague and slow, selector-wise, as you can get.

However, my advice in this regard would always be to test these assumptions. Selectors themselves are incredibly fast. It's generally the declarations within them that slow paint times but test this for yourself on your own style sheets. For those unfamiliar with Chrome's developer tools I would recommend starting at http://discover-devtools.codeschool.com/. With that knowledge it will be possible to test performance rather than rely on generalizations that are, you know, general, and may not apply to your situation.

Summary

In this chapter, we have learnt how to create and hopefully understand a very useful media query mixin that will give us the ability to insert media queries inline alongside the other styles that relate to the selector.

In addition, we have considered, tested, and quashed the performance arguments against using media queries in this manner.

Finally, we have taken the time to look at reviewing the CSS we are generating and think about some common problems that could be missed if just looking at the Sass files alone.

Out test site is looking a little healthier at various viewports now. However, it's still a little spartan (as in the empty and plain sense of the word, not the wearing sandals and swinging a sword kind).

In the next chapter, we're going to spice things up a little and see how easy it is to add cross-vendor box-shadows, gradients, and all kinds of crazy. Let's get to it.

7
Easy CSS3, Image Sprites, and More with Compass

Throughout the earlier chapters, we have used Compass lightly and sporadically. Although we used a number of Compass's amazing color features (such as `tint` and `shade`) in *Chapter 4, Manipulate Color with Ease*, we haven't explored the 'meat and potatoes' of what I feel makes Compass so useful.

Some of the most impressive and time-saving benefits of using Compass are its plethora of mixins for generating cross-browser experimental CSS styles. If that wasn't enough, Compass can also perform voodoo tricks such as automatically creating image sprites and data URIs from separate images.

In this chapter we are going to apply a whole load of Compass mixins and helpers to our `http://sassandcompass.com` project. Hopefully, this chapter should also serve as a handy reference for the syntaxes you'll need when using the most common Compass mixins day-to-day.

In this chapter, we will:

- Learn the Compass syntaxes for CSS features including box-shadow, text-shadow, background gradients, multiple columns, filters, and more
- Learn how to reference images with Compass's `image-url` helper
- Understand and control the Compass cache buster
- Learn how to automatically make an image sprite from a number of separate images
- Understand Compass's text-replacement features
- Use the Compass `inline-image` helper to embed small images as data URIs into the style sheet
- Learn the Compass mixins for easy CSS transforms
- Understand the Compass mixins for CSS transitions

Easy CSS3 with Compass's mixins

Compass has gained fast and fervent favor with developers as it enables authors to write a mixin using a single syntax that, on compile, generates a full vendor-prefixed 'stack' of properties in the CSS. This has been particularly useful with experimental CSS properties, often referred to in recent years as CSS3.

 CSS actually gets developed in modules so it is often possible that some modules are further along than others. Selectors, for example, is already a level 4 working draft specification: `http://www.w3.org/TR/selectors4/`.

Let's look at some of these common experimental properties and how we can produce cross-browser code with a relevant Compass mixin.

First up, `text-shadow`.

The text-shadow syntax

Text shadow is actually well supported in all modern browsers (Internet Explorer 9 being a notable exception), so Compass won't generate a vendor-prefixed stack for it (it's smart enough to know it isn't needed). Despite this, let's use a Compass mixin to include a shadow on our headline style.

 I have added the FitText.js jQuery plugin by the venerable Dave Rupert (`http://fittextjs.com/`) into the `plugin.js` file—this just lets the text scale and fills the area provided. When viewport-relative units are supported cross-browser (more info on those here: `http://www.w3.org/TR/css3-values/#viewport-relative-lengths`), this shouldn't be necessary.

We'll likely include this style on a few classes, so it's going into the `_placeholder.scss` file. Just remember that if the CSS will be used by someone else, it may be better to include the style directly, rather than extending a placeholder:

```
%headline-text-shadow {
  @include text-shadow(3px 4px 0px darken($color11,20%));
}
```

Then it can be extended as and when needed. For example:

```
.headline-hero {
  @extend %font-lobster;
  @extend %headline-text-shadow;
  font-size: 3.5em;
}
```

In case you're not familiar with the `text-shadow` syntax, let's define the different arguments it takes. After including the mixin, the first argument is for horizontal offset (a positive value creates a right-hand shadow, a negative value would create a shadow to the left). The second argument is for vertical offset (a positive value creates a bottom shadow, a negative value creates a top shadow). The third argument is for the amount of blur, and then the final argument is for the color of the shadow. You'll notice in this example that a Compass color manipulation is being used for the color argument but a hex value or CSS color name could be passed instead.

Take a look at the generated CSS and you'll notice that the CSS is pretty much what we have already written:

```
.ampersand, .headline-hero, .headline-sidekick {
  text-shadow: 3px 4px 0px #cccccc;
}
```

Text shadow with default values

To apply many identical text-shadows without using `@extend`, it's also possible to set some default variables for mixin. Although these are Compass-specific text shadow variables, they can live with the other variables with no ill effect:

```
$default-text-shadow-color: darken($color11,20%);
$default-text-shadow-blur: 0px;
$default-text-shadow-v-offset: 4px;
$default-text-shadow-h-offset: 3px;
```

Then, if not extending an existing placeholder style, a text-shadow could be applied to an element using the mixin like this:

```
@include text-shadow;
```

There's no need to pass any arguments to the mixin as it uses the defaults set by the variables (just amend those variables mentioned previously to suit your needs).

Here's the result in the browser:

To add multiple text-shadows to an element, just comma-separate each shadow. Here's an example of the syntax (warning, looking at the result of this may make your eyes bleed):

```
@include text-shadow(1px 1px 2px cyan, -2px -2px -3px blue);
```

The border-radius syntax

Border-radius is another CSS property that's finally settling down and being implemented sans vendor prefix in modern browsers. Regardless, to ensure the widest compatibility, use the Compass `border-radius` mixin. Here's an example:

```
@include border-radius(5px);
```

This applies the same radius to every corner of a box. We can set a variable as the default for the `border-radius` like this:

```
$default-border-radius: 5px;
```

Let's add that into our `_variables.scss` partial and then we can just include a rounded corner on an element like this:

```
@include border-radius;
```

That's fine when we need the same radius on every corner, but let's consider how we specify different radiuses for each corner:

```
@include border-top-right-radius(5px);
@include border-bottom-right-radius(5px);
@include border-bottom-left-radius(5px);
@include border-top-left-radius(5px);
```

Or, you can specify two continuous corners at once like this:

```
@include border-top-radius(5px); // top left and top right
@include border-right-radius(5px); // top right and bottom right
@include border-bottom-radius(5px); // bottom right and bottom left
@include border-left-radius(5px); // bottom left and bottom right
```

I'm sure we don't need to labor over those at it's really straightforward. Just include the mixin and pass the radius you want (if not the default) in parenthesis. Here is an example of the generated CSS produced from using `@include border-radius(5px)`:

```
-webkit-border-radius: 5px;
-moz-border-radius: 5px;
-ms-border-radius: 5px;
-o-border-radius: 5px;
border-radius: 5px;
```

Multiple columns

The CSS **Multi-column Layout Module** (`http://www.w3.org/TR/css3-multicol/`) specifies how an author can display content within an element across a number of columns. Compass has a mixin to produce the necessary cross-browser code. I'll be honest, this isn't something I use very often (with large amounts of text you have to scroll down and then back up to carry on reading which feels wonky), but it's nice to have regardless. We'll add an HTML class to the second paragraph of our markup and then use this mixin:

```
.two-cols {
  @include column-count(3);
}
```

Here is the effect in the browser:

Learn how to easily write more maintainable CSS with the Sass preprocessor and it's companion authoring framework Compass.

Whilst Sass and Compass may initially seem complex this book clearly explains the core concepts and tools in layman's terms (if you can write CSS and HTML, you can easily master Sass and Compass) so that you can get to grips with the awesome power of Sass and Compass and start writing CSS that is more modular, maintainable and easier to write than ever before.

We can amend this further by adding in a dividing rule like this:

```
.two-cols {
  @include column-count(3);
  @include column-rule(1px, dotted, lighten($color10, 84%));
}
```

Column rule syntax

The syntax for the arguments of the column rule mixin are the same as a CSS border; first the width of the dividing line, then the type of line, and finally the color, each separated with a comma.

Here is the effect of the prior mixin in the browser:

Learn how to easily write more maintainable CSS with the Sass preprocessor and it's companion authoring framework Compass.

Whilst Sass and Compass may initially seem complex this book clearly explains the core concepts and tools in layman's terms (if you can write CSS and HTML, you can easily master Sass and Compass) so that you can get to grips with the awesome power of Sass and Compass and start writing CSS that is more modular, maintainable and easier to write than ever before.

The Box Shadow mixin

Like `text-shadow`, there are a couple of ways we can implement box-shadows with Compass. The first is using defaults set as variables. Consider this:

```
$default-box-shadow-color: lighten($color10, 50%);
$default-box-shadow-h-offset: 1px;
$default-box-shadow-v-offset: 1px;
$default-box-shadow-blur: 2px;
$default-box-shadow-spread: false;
$default-box-shadow-inset: false;
```

With those variables in place (again, just place them alongside all the other variables you have), we can use the following mixin:

```
@include box-shadow;
```

Here, we're adding the `box-shadow` mixin to the header links. Here's the result in the browser:

If not using variables, it's possible to add a box-shadow like this (this is exactly the same shadow as before so hopefully the values make sense), by passing the arguments directly to the mixin:

```
@include box-shadow(1px 1px 2px lighten($color10, 50%));
```

The box-shadow syntax

The order of the arguments accepted by the `box-shadow` mixin is: inset (optional and omitted above), horizontal offset, vertical offset, blur, spread (optional and omitted above), and color. Like `text-shadow`, using a negative value on the offsets sends the shadow in the opposite direction.

Multiple box-shadows

To add a number of box-shadows concurrently, we just comma separate the box-shadows.

For example, let's keep the same style box-shadow on those buttons but also add an inset shadow at the top of the buttons. At this point, we'll amend the color of the buttons too for the purpose of showing the effect:

```
@include box-shadow(1px 1px 2px 0px lighten($color10, 50%),inset 0px
1px 0px 1px transparentize($color11, .5));
```

Remember that whenever color manipulations are being used with these mixins, the values could also be passed with a variable or standard color (using name, hex, or RGB/HSL value) instead. Just use whatever works best for you. To exemplify this, the previous code could be written as follows (assuming the relevant colors are set to the variable names being used) using variables instead:

```
@include box-shadow(1px 1px 2px 0px $a-color,inset
0px 1px 0px 1px $another-color);
```

Or if you want to use color and RGB values, it could be written like this:

```
@include box-shadow(1px 1px 2px 0px gray,inset 0px 1px 0px 1px
rgba(255,255,255,0.5));
```

However, once the color values are passed; here is the CSS generated:

```
-webkit-box-shadow: 1px 1px 2px 0px gray, inset 0px 1px 0px 1px
rgba(255, 255, 255, 0.5);
  -moz-box-shadow: 1px 1px 2px 0px gray, inset 0px 1px 0px 1px
rgba(255, 255, 255, 0.5);
    box-shadow: 1px 1px 2px 0px gray, inset 0px 1px 0px 1px rgba(255,
255, 255, 0.5);
```

The box-shadow mixin syntax follows the W3C box-shadow syntax (http://www.w3.org/TR/css3-background/#box-shadow). You can add as many box-shadows as you realistically need this way—just add another comma and add the next box-shadow. Here's what that prior code gives us in the browser:

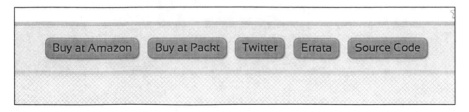

I think we can all agree that color (and my apologies if you are reading the hard copy of this sans color) looks awful but hopefully you can see the effect there. Let's remove the box-shadow now.

Perhaps we could put the box-shadow effect to better use on the `blockquote` area. I'm going to create a variable for the background color of the `blockquote` area and then use variations of that new color using the color adjustments we learned in *Chapter 4, Manipulate Color with Ease*. Here is the part relevant to the `box-shadow` mixin:

```
@include box-shadow(inset 0px 0px 20px transparentize(darken($blockquo
te-bg, 70%),.8));
```

And here is what that gives us in the browser:

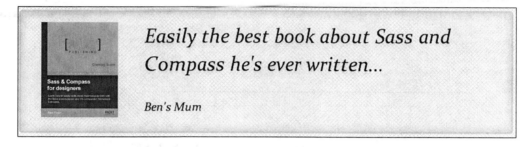

More importantly, here is the CSS generated for the box-shadow:

```
-webkit-box-shadow: inset 0px 0px 20px rgba(77, 59, 6, 0.2);
 -moz-box-shadow: inset 0px 0px 20px rgba(77, 59, 6, 0.2);
 box-shadow: inset 0px 0px 20px rgba(77, 59, 6, 0.2);
```

If you are interested in changing which vendor prefixes are created for experimental CSS properties, then this is covered in depth in *Chapter 9, Becoming a Sass and Compass Power User*.

Background gradients

If you've dealt with background-gradients for any length of time, you'll know there was a time of madness where we needed to write gazillions of different syntaxes in the CSS to ensure cross-browser compatibility. Thankfully, Compass lets us write one mixin with a single syntax and it produces all the necessary CSS to make browsers happy. Let's use this to spruce up the main header area. Currently we have a solid background color and a border below. Let's remove this and instead use a single background gradient and box shadow. Here are the two mixins being used:

```
@include background(linear-gradient(to bottom, darken($color-pink,
10%) 0px, darken($color-pink, 10%) 4px, lighten(complement($color-
pink), 10%) 4px,  complement($color-pink) 100%));
@include box-shadow(#ccc 0px 3px 10px);
```

Here is how that looks in the browser:

Background linear-gradient syntax

I'm aware that with all the color functions in that prior chunk of code, the `background` mixin syntax looks a little crazy. Here is an expanded explanation of the `background` mixin syntax with a linear gradient:

```
@include background(linear-gradient(to-direction, first-color first-
color-stop, second-color second-color-stop);
```

After passing the gradient type (we've used a linear gradient in this example, read on for the radial example), open parenthesis and first declare the 'to' or start direction for the gradient (it's also possible to define a start point as a degree value such as `90deg` too). Then, add the colors and stop locations, each separated by commas (with just a space delimiting the color and stop location).

The terms used to define the direction a linear gradient travels in changed fairly late in the development of the official specification. For example, it used to be top if you wanted a gradient to start at the top and head to the bottom. However, the official syntax is now to write `to bottom` in this situation instead.

If using a degree to define the direction a gradient travels in, be aware that `0deg` now means up and `90deg` means right. With Compass, at the time of writing, in most instances you can actually write it either way and Compass will figure it out. However, for best results, it makes sense to follow the official syntax: `http://www.w3.org/TR/css3-images/#linear-gradients`.

Here's another example with names to define the color values to simplify the syntax. Here the gradient starts at the left (and heads to the right):

```
@include background(linear-gradient(to right, blue 0px, purple 40px,
orange 150px, red 100%));
```

This is what it produces in the browser:

Background radial-gradient syntax

Here's an example of the background-image radial-gradient syntax:

```
@include background-image(radial-gradient(100% circle, pink 15%, red
100%));
```

The colors and stops syntax works the same as a linear gradient. The start position
is set as center if omitted (as in this example) so the first value given here within
parenthesis is the size of the circle (100% in this example). If wanted, ellipse could
have been used instead of circle. Next the colors and stops are defined in the same
manner as linear-gradients. The W3C reference for the radial-gradient syntax
can be found at http://www.w3.org/TR/css3-images/#radial-gradients.

 Don't forget that with gradients you can mix pixel values
and percentages for the color stops.

Combining background images and gradients

As you'll know, it's possible to have both background images and CSS background
gradients on an element. When we define the items in the background syntax, the
first element declared sits on the 'top' of the others. Let's add a repeating line graphic
on the header on top of the previous background gradient. We can use the Compass
image-url helper to link to it:

```
@include background(image-url("line.png"),linear-gradient(to
bottom, darken($color-pink, 10%) 0px, darken($color-pink, 10%) 4px,
lighten(complement($color-pink), 10%) 4px,  complement($color-pink)
100%));
```

Remember, if you wanted to, you could make variables for each of the color
conversions so the background looks cleaner. Here is the same thing done that way:

```
$dark-pink10: darken($color-pink, 10%);
$light-comp-pink: lighten(complement($color-pink), 10%);
$comp-pink: complement($color-pink);

@include background(image-url("line.png"),linear-gradient(to bottom,
$dark-pink10 0px, $dark-pink10 4px, $light-comp-pink 4px, $comp-pink
100%));
```

However you would rather do it, here is the generated CSS, with the usual vendor prefixes:

```
background: url('../img/line.png?1357945655'), -webkit-
gradient(linear, to bottom, to top, color-stop(0px, #ff8da1), color-
stop(5px, #ff8da1), color-stop(5px, #f3fffd), color-stop(100%,
#c0fff4));
   background: url('../img/line.png?1357945655'), -webkit-linear-
gradient(to bottom, #ff8da1 0px, #ff8da1 5px, #f3fffd 5px, #c0fff4
100%);
   background: url('../img/line.png?1357945655'), -moz-linear-
gradient(to bottom, #ff8da1 0px, #ff8da1 5px, #f3fffd 5px, #c0fff4
100%);
   background: url('../img/line.png?1357945655'), -o-linear-gradient(to
bottom, #ff8da1 0px, #ff8da1 5px, #f3fffd 5px, #c0fff4 100%);
   background: url('../img/line.png?1357945655'), linear-gradient(to
bottom, #ff8da1 0px, #ff8da1 5px, #f3fffd 5px, #c0fff4 100%);
```

Here is the effect of that in the browser:

Sass & Compass for designers

Hopefully you can see that, a sort of pin stripe repeated across the header.

 It's also possible to add another gradient, image, or flat color behind. Just add a comma after the existing gradient ends and list the next item.

Adding background images with the Compass image-url helper

With CSS, when you want to use a background image, it's usually necessary to provide the relative path to the image from the CSS. Here's an example:

```
background-image: url("../img/amazon-com.svg");
```

If you're anything like me, there's often a 'hunt the image path' game that happens on a new project, caused by trying to figure out and set the correct path to the image. For example, is the path to the images `../img/`, `./img`, `/img`, or just `img`? Thankfully, with Compass the `image-url` helper has us covered. Remember back in *Chapter 2, Setting Up a Sass and Compass project*, we looked at the `config.rb` file. One of the configuration options we set was this:

```
images_dir = "img"
```

This lets us target images for backgrounds easily from within our Sass files, no matter where they are in our project. It doesn't matter whether a style is buried in a partial file three 'levels' away from the image, we can still just do this:

```
background-image: image-url("amazon-com.svg");
```

Just specify `image-url`, open parenthesis, and then provide the name of the image in the relevant folder you want to link to. Compass does the smart linking and produces the appropriate path to the image in the compiled CSS.

Image width and height helpers

There are also a couple of image helpers for automatically determining an image's height or width. Therefore, as long as we're not using SVG images (as they are vector-based they can have indeterminate dimensions), we can use these helpers to automatically get and set the height and width of appropriate CSS properties:

```
.buy-amazon-uk {
  display: block;
  background-image: image-url("amazon-co-uk.png");
  background-size: image-width("amazon-co-uk.png") image-height("amazon-co-uk.png");
  background-position: 50% 50%;
  background-repeat: no-repeat;
  height: image-height("amazon-co-uk.png");
  width: image-width("amazon-co-uk.png");
}
```

In this example, we are using these helpers to not only set the `background-size` property but also set the image width and height. Here's the relevant CSS that compiles to:

```
.buy-amazon-uk {
  background-image: url('../img/amazon-co-uk.png?1357598801');
  background-size: 223px 50px;
  background-position: 50% 50%;
  background-repeat: no-repeat;
  height: 50px;
  width: 223px;
}
```

The Compass cache buster

You may be wondering what that funny string of numbers is for at the end of the PNG filename here:

```
background-image: url('../img/amazon-co-uk.png?1357598801');
```

It's the Compass **cache buster**; it prevents browsers caching assets when they have changed (the value changes each time the image's modification time changes). It's more Compass-automatic goodness. To disable it on a case-by-case basis you can do this:

```
background-image: image-url("amazon-co-uk.png", false, false);
```

After the image name, the first `false` is for the `url()` function. If this is set to `true`, only the path to the image is written out. To illustrate, it would compile to this:

```
background-image: ../img/amazon-co-uk.png;
```

Which isn't a whole lot of use as it's invalid CSS! There are obviously situations where this might be useful but this example isn't it!

The second `false` is what turns the cache buster off (should you need to).

 There's a number of other Compass helpers, you can view the full list at http://compass-style.org/reference/compass/helpers/.

Compass image sprites

While we can set the background images for elements with the help of Compass image helpers for individual images, it's often considered a better practice to use an image sprite. I'm sure you'll have used this technique before. A single image (referred to as an 'image sprite') is created that includes all the other images. This single image is then shifted around by the CSS `background-position` property to show different images on different elements. The technique has an additional benefit of using images for hover states. As the single image is already loaded, there's no delay when an item is hovered over (the delay is usually caused by the separate hover image being requested, fetched, and parsed).

It's a great technique but not without some headaches, principally, working out the background positions for each image. Well, guess what? Compass can take care of all this and more. I hope you're sitting down. This is quite simply brilliant.

We will use this technique to set the background images for all the purchase links at the bottom of our site. There are four images needed, one for `Amazon.com`, one for Barnes and Noble, another for `Amazon.co.uk`, and a final one for Packt Publishing (the publishers of this fine tome you are currently enjoying/enduring).

First of all, we need to create a folder to contain all the images from which we want to create an image sprite. Let's make a folder called `buy-sprite` within `img` and place the images within (they all need to be PNG image files for this to work). The four files being added into that folder are named `amazon-us.png`, `amazon-uk.png`, `barnes-and-noble.png`, and `packt.png`.

> **Add the oily_png gem**
>
> Although not essential, Compass can produce sprite sheets a little faster if `oily_png` is installed. To install this gem, run `gem install oily_png` from the command line.

Now in the `_modules.scss` partial we can add this:

```
@import "buy /*.png";
@include all-buy-sprites;
```

Two things are going on here. The first `@import` statement is telling Compass to import all PNG images that live in the `buy` folder.

The `@include` statement that follows adheres to the following syntax: `all` tells Compass we want a sprite of all the images. Then there is a dash and then the name of the folder that the image files currently reside in; in our example, the folder name is `buy`. Finally, after the second dash, we simply tell Compass that we want to include these images as sprites.

On compile, here is what those two lines of Compass-powered Sass generate into CSS:

```css
.buy-sprite, .buy-amazon-uk, .buy-amazon-us, .buy-barnes-and-noble,
.buy-packt {
  background: url('../img/buy-sef1373fa31.png') no-repeat;
}

.buy-amazon-uk {
  background-position: 0 0;
}

.buy-amazon-us {
  background-position: 0 -100px;
}

.buy-barnes-and-noble {
  background-position: 0 -50px;
}

.buy-packt {
  background-position: 0 -150px;
}
```

Compass has created an image sprite for us and automatically created a number of CSS selectors (based upon the name of the images and the folder they reside in) with relevant styles for the appropriate background position. To illustrate how we can now use this, consider the HTML classes we added to the purchase links in the markup:

```html
<a class="buy-barnes-and-noble ir" href="http://barnesandnoble.
com">Barnes and Noble</a>
```

Because of this, we'll automatically get the background images on these elements. However, we'll need to set the height and width for these elements; otherwise we won't get to see the relevant area of the image sprite behind. One way to remedy that is by adding this:

```scss
// Create a variable for width and height based on the individual
images
$buy-height: buy-sprite-height(amazon-uk);
$buy-width: buy-sprite-width(amazon-uk);
```

We are creating a variable and then setting the value of the variable with the help of a Compass sprite helper.

Here's the syntax of that helper. First, the name of the folder the images are in (buy in our example), then the sprite (as we want to get the dimension of an image within the sprite), and then the dimension we want (height or width). Then, in parenthesis is the image within the sprite we want to get the dimensions from (the image called amazon-uk in this instance). Then we can use these variables to set the width and height like this:

```
// Set the width and height for the elements that need to show the
background images
[class^="buy-"] {
  @extend %block;
  height: $buy-height;
  width: $buy-width;
}
```

And that extra section compiles to this CSS:

```
[class^="buy-"] {
  height: 34px;
  width: 150px;
}
```

With that in place, here's what we get in the browser:

Ignore the text showing above the sprite for now. We'll deal with that shortly!

The preceding technique might not be a perfect solution if the images were different sizes. Thankfully Compass can sort this out for us with some additional configuration options.

To take effect, the variables for additional configuration options should be included before the import directive that produces the sprite sheet.

Additional sprite configuration options

There are a number of additional configuration options that you can pass to Compass that affect the way a sprite is produced. Let's look at a couple of the most useful now.

Add the height and width to each generated HTML selector

To automatically have the `width` and `height` properties produced for each HTML selector class and rules, add this variable:

```
$buy-sprite-dimensions: true;
```

This compiles into rules, such as the following, for each sprite (again, `buy` in that variable is the name of the folder containing the images so change this to suit your needs):

```
.buy-amazon-us {
  background-position: 0 -54px;
  height: 34px;
  width: 150px;
}
```

Extra padding around the images

If extra space is needed around each image in the sprite, it can be done by adding this variable:

```
$buy-spacing: 10px;
```

Here, `buy` is the name of the folder where the images are stored and the value in pixels is the extra space needed. Just amend the spacing to suit.

 Although I've seldom (if ever) found any use for them, there are a few more configuration options for sprites; check them out here: http://compass-style.org/help/tutorials/ spriting/customization-options/.

Layout options

If Compass hadn't already done enough for us, it also includes the ability to control how the image sprite is produced. For example, whether the images are stacked vertically, horizontally, diagonally, or 'smartly' in the sprite.

This can be a big help if trying to use sprites for a number of horizontal navigation icons, for example. It makes more sense to have a vertical sprite sheet so there is less chance of one background icon impinging upon another. It's all set with the following variable:

```
$buy-layout: horizontal;
```

Here, `buy` is the name of the folder where the images are stored. That example arranges the images horizontally. Use `vertical` for vertically arranged images:

```
$buy-layout: vertical;
```

Here's the variable for diagonally-orientated images in the sprite:

```
$buy-layout: diagonal;
```

Be aware that the Compass documentation notes that `diagonal` is the most resource-intensive for the browser (meaning it has to work harder to shift the sprite around), while the `final` option is the least resource-intensive for the browser:

```
$buy-layout: smart;
```

The `smart` layout places each image where it best fits.

Now, the fact that the original text is still showing on top of the background images we have made with the sprites isn't lost on me. Thankfully, Compass has us covered here too.

Compass's text replacement mixins

Compass has a few mixins to help deal with occasions when you want to hide text. Let's look at some of those.

The hide-text mixin

The first one we'll look at is the `hide-text` mixin. This is how it looks:

```
@include hide-text;
```

Here's an example of how you would use it:

```
.hide-text {
  @include hide-text;
}
```

Here's the CSS it produces:

```
.hide-text {
  text-indent: -119988px;
  overflow: hidden;
  text-align: left;
}
```

Now, that certainly gets the job done. If the `@include hide-text` mixin is added to the `ir` selector, it shifts the text accordingly. However, be aware that to do this, the browser is painting a box with the text in `119988px` off the screen. That's not really an issue on desktop machines but it may be on mobile devices. Some alternative techniques are listed as follows, however, for now, here is the effect in the browser:

The squish-text mixin

Compass also has a mixin called `squish-text` to squish text inline if you want it to be visually hidden but still accessible to screen readers. Here's the mixin:

```
@include squish-text;
```

We can apply that instead of the previous `hide-text` mixin:

```
.ir {
  @include squish-text;
}
```

And this creates the following CSS:

```
.ir {
  font: 0/0 serif;
  text-shadow: none;
  color: transparent;
}
```

While this has the same visual effect as the preceding example in modern browsers, it's most useful for hiding inline text. As an example, we could amend the markup, wrapping relevant sections in an inline element (span, b, or i, for example) with this class applied. For example:

```
<p class="two-cols">Whilst <span class="squish-text">Sass and </
span>Compass may initially seem complex this book clearly explains
the core concepts and tools in layman's terms (if you can write CSS
and HTML, you can easily master <span class="squish-text">Sass and </
span>Compass) so that you can get to grips with the awesome power of
<span class="squish-text">Sass and </span>Compass and start writing
CSS that is more modular, maintainable and easier to write than ever
before.</p>
```

While screen readers and other assistive technologies can 'read' that text, here is the visual effect in the browser:

> Whilst Compass may initially seem complex this book clearly explains the core concepts and tools in layman's terms (if you can write CSS and HTML, you can easily master Compass) so that you can get to grips with the awesome power of Compass and start writing CSS that is more modular, maintainable and easier to write than ever before.

It suffices to say, you could have a lot of fun altering the meaning of text with this technique!

Replace text with image dimensions

If not using an image sprite for backgrounds, there is another Compass mixin that is really handy for showing an image instead of text. It's useful when wanting a logo in place of a header tag for example.

The key benefit is that it automatically sets the dimensions of the element according to the size of the image being used. Here is the aptly named replace-text-with-image-dimensions mixin:

```
@include replace-text-with-dimensions('image.png');
```

To exemplify, we can add this to the ir selector's styles:

```
.ir {
  @include replace-text-with-dimensions('buy/amazon-uk.png');
}
```

And here is the generated CSS:

```
.ir {
  text-indent: -119988px;
  overflow: hidden;
  text-align: left;
  background-image: url('../img/buy/amazon-uk.png?1357685584');
  background-repeat: no-repeat;
  background-position: 50% 50%;
  width: 150px;
  height: 34px;
}
```

You can see here that it has added the correct link to the image and also set the width and height to the correct size. Thanks Compass!

Yet more image replacement techniques

There has been a number of text replacement techniques over the years. The currently accepted gold standard is the one employed in the HTML5 Boilerplate project (http://html5boilerplate.com). In case you're interested, the HTML5 boilerplate image replacement styles are included in the _chapter-examples.scss partial for this chapter. You can also view the HTML5 Boilerplate at their GitHub repository here: https://github.com/h5bp/html5-boilerplate.

Creating data URIs from images

One problem with PNG-based image sprites is that they are not resolution independent. With more and more HiDPI devices (Apple gives their HiDPI devices the 'retina' moniker) coming onto the market, that necessitates us creating at least two sprites to cover normal and HiDPI devices. That situation will only get worse as higher and higher DPI devices enter the market and I, for one, don't like repetitive work!

Furthermore, the spriting technique we have already looked at doesn't play particularly well with responsive designs (as currently, the Compass image sprite engine uses pixel-based, rather than proportional, positioning) so they have fallen out of favor with me of late.

Instead, where possible, I opt for SVG images. As their name implies, (Scalable Vector Graphics—you knew that already though, I know) SVGs are entirely scalable and look incredibly sharp on all devices, regardless of pixel density.

Wondering how to produce SVGs? Adobe Illustrator handles them natively as does (the free) Inkscape (`http://inkscape.org/`). A lower cost alternative to Illustrator on OS X is Sketch by Bohemian Coding (`http://www.bohemiancoding.com/sketch/`).

I would also recommend the free SVG Edit (`https://code.google.com/p/svg-edit/`). It's browser-based but don't let that fool you. It produces compact and clean markup.

If you are a Fireworks user and want to export existing graphics as SVG, I would recommend Aaron Beall's free extension (although if it's useful, consider sending him a donation) at `http://fireworks.abeall.com/extensions/commands/Export/`.

Just be aware that if you need to support IE8 and below on the desktop and early (pre 2.3) Android devices you are out of luck when it comes to using native SVGs (my sympathies to you and your code). There are, however, SVG polyfills that may help if you are feeling particularly desperate. Have a look at `https://github.com/Modernizr/Modernizr/wiki/HTML5-Cross-browser-Polyfills`.

Now, you're perhaps wondering if SVGs are one step forward and two steps back. For example, we gain resolution independence but we still don't have the advantage of a single asset for all the background images, as we would with an image sprite.

It is possible to have an SVG-based sprite, just not made by Compass at present. Furthermore, I have found SVG sprites (using em-based values for background position) to be a little brittle cross-browser, Opera being a principal offender. At this point, therefore, I have a different recommendation.

SVG files, in comparison to bitmap formats (for example JPG, GIF, PNG) are typically far smaller. Therefore, to reduce the number of requests, we can convert the SVGs into data URIs (**Uniform Resource Identifier**) and include them inline with the rest of our CSS.

In case you have no idea what a data URI even is, it is the process of embedding a file into the code, negating the need to fetch a separate resource (such as an image in our instance). Sounds complicated? Not with Compass; it makes this process trivial.

More on data URIs

We haven't covered much on the whys and hows of data URIs here as it's a little beyond the scope of this book. However, for some good info on the subject, Nicholas C. Zakas wrote a good piece back in 2010 here: `http://www.nczonline.net/blog/2010/07/06/data-uris-make-css-sprites-obsolete/` (have a read of the comments too). Also, if you want to test the relative speed of data URIs and standard background images for your own assets, your humble author documented this step-by-step: `http://benfra.in/1z7`.

The inline-image syntax

Here is the `inline-image` syntax:

```
background-image: inline-image("svg/amazon-us.svg");
```

In this instance, the SVG has been placed within a subfolder of the `img` folder (hence the additional path to the SVG).

Here's the start of the CSS generated by that rule (truncated for brevity):

```
.buy-amazon-us {
  background-image: url('data:image/svg+xml;base64,PD94bWwgdmVy
c2lvbj0iMS4wIiBlbmNvZGluZz0idXRmLTgiPz4NCjwhLS0gR2VuZXJhdG9yOiB
BZG9iZSBJbGx1c3RyYXRvciAxNi4wLjMsIFNWRy
```

Extending this technique to our purchase links, here is the code we can use:

```
[class^="buy-"] {
  @extend %block;
  min-height: 2.5em;
  background-position: 50% 50%;
  background-size: contain;
  background-repeat: no-repeat;
}

.buy-amazon-us {
  background-image: inline-image("svg/amazon-us.svg");
}
.buy-amazon-uk {
  background-image: inline-image("svg/amazon-uk.svg");
}
```

```
.buy-barnes-and-noble {
  background-image: inline-image("svg/barnes-and-noble.svg");
}
.buy-packt {
  background-image: inline-image("svg/packt.svg");
}

.ir {
  @include hide-text;
}
```

And here is the effect in the browser:

Nice! Resolution-independent images. In a few years, time when I'm ego surfing this site on my iPhone 8S with an 800ppi pixel density, those SVGs will still look great!

Easy fallbacks for non-SVG capable devices

Thanks to the Sass parent selector we've already learned about in *Chapter 3, Nesting, Extend, Placeholders, and Mixins*, remember that it's easy to create fallbacks in tandem with Modernizr for different device capabilities. For example, although opting for SVGs as default, we could provide a fallback to equivalent PNG graphics, like this:

```
.buy-amazon-us {
  background-image: inline-image("svg/amazon-us.svg");
  .no-svg & {
    background-image: image-url("png/amazon-us.png");
  }
}
```

Bet on SVG!

SVG is currently an underused technology on the Web, but there are is a host of exciting features hopefully coming to it in the near future, fragment identifiers (http://www.broken-links.com/2012/08/14/better-svg-sprites-with-fragment-identifiers/) being but one example.

CSS transforms

Compass has a mixin for defining any CSS Level 3 transform.

The Compass 2D transform mixins follow exactly the same syntax as the W3C 2D Transform Functions (http://www.w3.org/TR/css3-transforms/#two-d-transform-functions).

Therefore, if we wanted to scale we could write this:

```
@include scale(2,2); // Make it twice original size
```

If we wanted to translate (translate moves an element in 2D space) we could write this:

```
@include translateX(20px); // Move it 20px right
```

For the odd occasions when you want to add multiple transforms to a single element, use the `simple-transform` mixin. Here's an example:

```
@include simple-transform(1.05,3deg);
```

That would scale the image by `1.05` and also rotate it by `3` degrees. The arguments must be passed in this order: `scale`, `rotate`, `translate-x`, `translate-y`, `skew-x`, `skew-y`, `origin-x`, `origin-y`. However, just remember this is only really useful for combining multiple transforms. Ordinarily, for a single transform, just use the standard transform mixins already described.

To put one of these transforms to good use, in the chapter code you'll see that I'm using a `rotate` mixin on a pseudo element. This is taking an absolutely-positioned box and rotating it. By aligning this rotated box, it will give the appearance of a triangle along the edge of another box. In this case it's to indicate which of the pages a user is currently on.

Here's the code for the `rotate` mixin:

```
@include rotate(45deg);
```

If you want to see the other styles in use, look at the chapter code—it's being applied to the `:after` pseudo element of `.chapter-summary`. The following screenshot shows how the styles render in the browser:

Now, there are times when we need a shadow around things that don't want a shadow around them. For example, let's suppose that instead of a rotated square, we wanted an isosceles triangle. We could make that with CSS borders (don't overthink it, just head over to `http://apps.eky.hk/css-triangle-generator/`). Here is the general amended code for the pseudo element:

```
&:before {
  content:"\00a0";
  position: absolute;
  width: 0px;
  height: 0px;
  top: 50%;
  right: 0%;
  margin-top: -5px;
```

```
    margin-right: -10px;
  }
  &:after {
    content:"\00a0";
    position: absolute;
    width: 0px;
    height: 0px;
    top: 50%;
    right: 0%;
    margin-top: -4px;
    margin-right: -8px;
  }
```

We're using two pseudo elements to produce the highlighted effect (one larger one, positioned directly behind the other). The chapter's code details the colors used for the gradient and borders. That's not particularly interesting to us here. All we need to see is the problem we have in the browser with this technique. Have a look at this screenshot:

Although it's visually a triangle, it still lives in a box as far as CSS is concerned. And the box-shadow is being applied to that box. Fear not, when bosses and/or clients demand shadows around irregular shapes, we can use Compass to provide access to the new CSS Filters. That might solve this issue.

> Be aware that in the real world a better solution to this problem would probably be to make the triangle shape with an icon-font and then use a standard text-shadow but then I wouldn't have been able to share all this fun stuff with you.

CSS Filters

Compass provides a mixin to produce a vendor-prefixed stack of properties for CSS Filters. The syntax follows the W3C specification described here at `http://www.w3.org/TR/filter-effects/`.

Let's use the `drop-shadow` filter to solve our prior issue. We'll remove the existing `box-shadow` mixin and instead apply a CSS `drop-shadow` filter with the Compass mixin:

```
@include filter(drop-shadow(#ccc 1px 1px 0px));
```

And here is the effect in the browser:

Compass will let you apply all CSS filters in this manner, essentially following the W3C syntax for the relevant filter.

Be aware that filters are experimental at this stage so you may find, as in this instance, that it leads to blurring of the text. I'm therefore reverting to the rotated square with the box-shadow technique we used before.

Transitions

One final Compass mixin to share with you is the **transitions** mixin. It allows an easy cross-browser way to use CSS transitions. Here's an example of the mixin in action:

```
@include single-transition(all, .3s, ease, 0s);
```

Again, it follows the same basic syntax as the W3C transition syntax (http://www.w3.org/TR/css3-transitions/).

Inside the parenthesis, the first value is the property to be transitioned (all in this instance), then the duration of the transition, next is the timing method (ease in this instance), and finally the transition delay. We'll add that to the header links to make a smooth transition to the hover-based styles.

As ever, Compass provides a full vendor-prefixed stack in the CSS, here's the output of the single-transition mixin we just wrote:

```
-webkit-transition: all 0.3s ease;
-webkit-transition-delay: 0s;
-moz-transition: all 0.3s ease 0s;
-o-transition: all 0.3s ease 0s;
transition: all 0.3s ease 0s;
```

 Compass will also let you deal with multiple transitions in one go although I'll be honest, I've never found the need. Should that madness prove essential, use @include transition(); and include each transition comma-separated within the parenthesis. For more on the possible Compass transitions, here is the official documentation: http://compass-style.org/reference/compass/css3/transition/.

Summary

In this chapter, we've used some of the many and varied helpers and mixins of Compass to significantly improve the aesthetics of our test project. We've created an image sprite, made data URIs, background gradients, shadows, and a whole lot more.

Hopefully, you are already realizing how much easier these tools and techniques can make your style sheet authoring. Remember, for the full list of Compass helpers and mixins, you can consult the Compass documentation at `http://compass-style.org/reference/compass/`.

In the next chapter, we'll concentrate on trying to make our existing code DRYer (a programming acronym for **Don't Repeat Yourself**), focusing on how we can use the programmatic power that Sass affords, to generate repetitive code more easily.

We shouldn't let words such as 'programmatic' and 'logic' worry us, though. We can totally do this!

 The Compass homepage is at `http://compass-style.org` and you can view the reference documentation for Compass features at `http://compass-style.org/reference/compass/`.

8
Programmatic Logic with Sass

In the last chapter, we used Compass to significantly improve the aesthetics of our design. Granted, there's still a lot of refining to do until it's something we can be proud of.

Despite this, rather than spend our remaining time tweaking existing values in the style sheets, let's demystify some of the seemingly impenetrable aspects of Sass—logic.

When it comes to writing style sheets, I believe I'm fairly pragmatic. Therefore, I am going to tell you straight away that in most instances you could get by just fine with no knowledge of the techniques we will look at in this chapter. Therefore, if you're happy to be mediocre, skip right ahead. I don't judge.

For those still reading I salute you. It means you want to be a Sass rock star. Excellent, that's the spirit. With that in mind, take a look at the amazing Ninja skills we will be using in this chapter:

- Math calculations with Sass
- Control directives and how to use them
- Learning what interpolation is and how we can use it
- Writing `if`, `for`, and `each` loops in Sass
- Stripping and adding units to variables
- Writing functions in Sass
- Using the `@debug` directive

Understanding and implementing logic with Sass is the equivalent of 'turning it up to 11' (kids, that's a Spinal Tap reference, ask your parents). Or, at the risk of stretching our earlier Karate Kid analogy to breaking point, here come the moves that are going to stun the baddies and win the girl (or guy).

Tie on your lucky headband and roll up your gi sleeves. Let's do this.

Math calculations with Sass

Sass can perform all manner of mathematical conversions. Let's look at some simple examples:

Addition

Here's addition:

```
.addition {
    width: 20% + 80%;
}
```

When this is compiled, it results in this:

```
.addition {
  width: 100%;
}
```

Subtraction

We can also do subtraction, multiplication, and division. Here's subtraction:

```
.subtraction {
    width: 80% - 20%;
}
```

Which compiles to this:

```
.subtraction {
  width: 60%;
}
```

Multiplication

When it comes to multiplication and division with Sass, there are a few considerations. Although Sass can support various units (for example em, px, %), when a unit is declared on both values it gets a little upset. This is the wrong way to do multiplication:

```
.multiplication {
    width: 20px * 80px;
}
```

Instead, you need to provide the units on just one value. For example, amend the prior example to this:

```
.multiplication {
    width: 20 * 80px;
}
```

This would compile as you might expect:

```
.multiplication {
  width: 1600px;
}
```

Division

Those same rules apply to division but as / is a symbol already used in CSS, it's necessary to remember that it will only be used as a division identifier if the values are enclosed in parenthesis. So, for example, if we used this:

```
.division {
    width: 80% / 20%;
}
```

We shouldn't be too surprised when our CSS compiles to this:

```
.division {
  width: 80%/20%;
}
```

Which is, you know, useless.

Instead, we can amend that to this:

```
.division {
    width: (80%/20);
}
```

And that will compile as expected:

```
.division {
  width: 4%;
}
```

Besides wrapping the calculation in parenthesis, the / symbol will also be interpreted as division if it is used as part of an existing piece of arithmetic. For example:

```
.addition-and-division {
    width: 20px + 80px / 5;
}
```

Now, if you're a math dunce like me, you may have been expecting that to compile with a value of 20 (20 plus 80 equals 100, divide by 5 is 20). However, it actually compiles to:

```
.addition-and-division {
    width: 36px;
}
```

This is because it actually divides 80px by 5 (giving a value of 16) and then adds that to 20, giving us 36px. To remedy this situation, you can employ parenthesis:

```
.addition-and-division-parenthesis {
    width: (20px + 80px) / 5;
}
```

This compiles how your mathematically challenged author expected:

```
.addition-and-division-parenthesis {
  width: 20px;
}
```

The Sass interactive shell

In the next chapter, we'll look at a way to perform calculations with Sass that doesn't require reading the compiled code to get the answer. It's called the **Sass interactive shell**. Yes, it's based in the command line but you'd better believe people will be impressed when they see you using it (in a very 1980s 'Wargames' kind of way)!

Calculations using variables

Now, so far, so 'what the hell are you showing me that my calculator can't do!' Well, first of all, we can use variables instead of values. This starts to make the mathematical capabilities of Sass a little more practical:

```
$main-width: 60%;
$sidebar-width: 40%;
$full-width: $main-width + $sidebar-width;

.main {
    width: $full-width;
}
```

Here, we're setting up three variables. One is for a sidebar, another for the main content and then a final one that is set to be the total of the previous two. Then, we are just using that final variable in a property and value pair. As you would expect, this is what the CSS compiles to:

```
.main {
  width: 100%;
}
```

It is obvious to see how this could start to be useful as values in the CSS can be the result of calculations rather than mere guesswork (I know, you never 'just guessed', me neither).

Control directives and how to use them

'Control directives' sounds a bit scientific — "Hank, initiate the control directives and fire up the hydro drives". However, it's actually a lot more straightforward than that. Control directives simply mean that Sass has functionality baked-in to control when styles get generated.

Remember in *Chapter 6, Advanced Media Queries with Sass and Mixins*, we looked at our MQ mixin and noted it was essentially a series of if statements (if this is true do this, otherwise do something else). That is an example of a control directive in Sass; it is controlling what is generated based on certain conditions. See? Easy.

Sass has a few of these control directives so let's look at some examples. Perhaps more importantly, how we could actually make use of them. How about a way to easily switch the theme of our site?

The @if and @else if control directives

Consider this:

```
$color-theme: orange;

@if $color-theme == pink {
  $color-brand: pink;
} @else if $color-theme == orange {
  $color-brand: #ff9900;
}
```

With this set, we can instantly switch the colors on our site. If you didn't like the pink hues we had before, I'm pretty sure this will make you queasy:

I know, what a looker! However, with that control directive in place we can easily revert the site to its prior 'festive' glory just by amending that one variable, like this:

```
$color-theme: pink;
```

As many of our existing colors are determined through relationships with one another, (for example, `complement`, `invert`, and so on that we learned about in *Chapter 4*, *Manipulate Color with Ease*) amending the value of this one variable changes the colors throughout the style sheet.

Needless to say, you can extend that example, adding extra @else if statements for as many color variations as needed.

 It's worth remembering that an @if statement can be followed by multiple @else if statements but only a single @else (listed at the end).

@for loops

Let's look at another control directive—the @for loop. This allows us to make virtually limitless styles.

Remember in the last chapter, when we made four styles with inline SVGs for the various 'buy' links (logos for Amazon, Barnes and Noble, and the like)? Well, with a little fore ward planning we can produce that kind of thing with a single @for loop, plus, also provide a fallback to PNG files for lesser browsers with the help of Modernizr.

In our current situation, at first glance the following piece of code may seem more difficult than simply writing the rules out as we would with 'vanilla' CSS (although even with just these 4 items, it reduces 24 lines of code in our Sass to 8).

However, what about if we had 10 rules to write? Or 100? Each with a tiny incremental difference. This is where the @for loop technique shines. It lets us make our code DRYer (remember that's an acronym for Don't Repeat Yourself).

Enough talk, let's give this control directive a whirl. We'll create our four 'buy' rules (and their PNG equivalent as a fallback for when SVG isn't supported) with one @for loop.

To accomplish this little task, first, we'll rename the various SVG and PNG images to have sequential numbers. For example, buy_1.svg, buy_2.svg, and so on. This will make more sense in a moment. We'll also need to rename the HTML classes (for example, from buy-packt to buy_4) in the markup to match.

Then we can write this in the Sass:

```
@for $i from 1 through 4 {

  .buy_#{$i} {

        background-image: image-url("svg/buy_#{$i}.svg");

        .no-svg & {

          background-image: image-url("buy/buy_#{$i}.png");

        }

    }

}
```

And that will produce this in the CSS:

```
.buy_1 {
  background-image: url('../img/svg/buy_1.svg?1357858329');
}
.no-svg .buy_1 {
  background-image: url('../img/buy/buy_1.png?1357685594');
}

.buy_2 {
  background-image: url('../img/svg/buy_2.svg?1357858011');
}
.no-svg .buy_2 {
  background-image: url('../img/buy/buy_2.png?1357685584');
}

.buy_3 {
  background-image: url('../img/svg/buy_3.svg?1357858078');
}
.no-svg .buy_3 {
  background-image: url('../img/buy/buy_3.png?1357685607');
}

.buy_4 {
  background-image: url('../img/svg/buy_4.svg?1357858103');
}
.no-svg .buy_4 {
  background-image: url('../img/buy/buy_4.png?1357685618');
}
```

Notice here that for this example, we've switched to referencing a background image rather than using a data URI. This is merely to make the example clearer. With smaller images such as these, in production, it often makes more sense to opt for a data URI.

Now we've done that, let's consider how the magic happened. Here's the first line:

```
@for $i from 1 through 4 {
```

The `@for` part is obvious, this merely indicates to Sass that we're beginning a `@for` loop. Then comes the 'counter' variable, in this case it's indicated with `$i`. If you've ever worked with something like PHP or JavaScript, this convention will be straightforward. For everyone else, here is all you need to know.

Understanding the counter variable

A counter variable is just a placeholder for the current state of the loop; it increments with each iteration of the loop. It might help to think of it like the odometer on a car that counts up with each passing mile on a journey. We don't actually see that variable change, it's merely a convention that we use in the places we want to 'print' the incrementing value.

Usually the variable used is called `$i` but it doesn't have to be, it can be anything you like — `$shazam`, or `$Daniel-san` if you'd rather. Just as long as it is unique. However, although you can name it differently, `$i` is a good choice as many programmers understand the convention and its compact, so it saves a few keystrokes.

In our example, it's inserting the incremented number in the places we have indicated. More on how we do that in a moment.

'From to' and 'from through'

After the counter variable we are providing a value in the `from` and `through` sections.

Now, using:

```
@for $i from 1 through 4 {
```

This gives us four loops, starting at 1 and ending at 4. However, the loop can also be made to go up to but not include the final number. This difference is achieved by switching the keyword through, to to. For, example:

```
@for $i from 1 to 4 {
```

That would give us only three iterations of the loop (ending when it gets to four). My advice would be to choose the @for version that suits the way you think and stick to it. When I've mixed and matched in the past, it got a bit messy and I wasn't the most fun guy to be around until I'd had a hazelnut latte and a slice of carrot cake (then I was incredible again, just ask my long suffering wife).

It's not necessary to always start at 1 either. You can alter the loop to your exact requirements. For example:

```
@for $i from 65 through 84 {
```

Would start iterating at 65 and end with 84.

That's the most difficult part of understanding @for loops covered. The only thing left to do is insert our placeholder where we need the iterated value to get 'printed'. We do that by a process known as **interpolation**.

Understanding interpolation

I know, interpolation is another of those terms that makes us sound like coneheads, "Commander, the interpolation is off the chart, we may need to abort". Thankfully, it has a simple-to-understand definition. It simply means to insert something into something else (interpolate your own joke here). Let's look at our loop again:

```
@for $i from 1 through 4 {
  .buy_#{$i} {
        background-image: image-url("svg/buy_#{$i}.svg");
        .no-svg & {
          background-image: image-url("buy/buy_#{$i}.png");
        }
    }
}
```

We've already wrapped our head around the loop and how we create our iteration ranges. The next weird-looking piece of code is this: `#{$i}`. This is interpolation. It's the process of inserting the value of a variable elsewhere in the Sass.

As you can see, here we are using it to 'print' the value of the counter variable in each iteration of the loop when the CSS is compiled. We're using interpolation in three places in our `@for` loop:

- To increment the buy HTML selector: `.buy_#{$i}`
- To increment the image number for the SVG: `svg/buy_#{$i}.svg`
- To increment the image number for the PNG: `buy/buy_#{$i}.png`

> While interpolation can be used to insert the value into selector names and image references, it can't be used to dynamically create variables (for example, interpolating a value onto the end of an existing variable). That's the Sass equivalent of 'crossing the streams' (kids, that's a Ghostbusters reference, ask someone older at the same time you ask about Spinal Tap).

Although the variable being used for interpolation in this loop is `$i`, interpolation could be used on any variable we have defined elsewhere to print its value out to the compiled CSS.

We'll use interpolation again in our next loop.

@each loops

In the previous tip we considered that it isn't possible to increment the name of variables within a loop. I had this fact confirmed by our friend Eric A. Meyer (of Susy fame) when I posed the question: `http://stackoverflow.com/questions/12863009/how-to-increment-a-variable-in-scss-with-a-for-loop/`

Instead, it was recommended to use an `@each` loop and that's the final type of control directive we'll look at.

The `@each` loop is useful for iterating through a list of items. An example will probably be useful here. Let's use an `@each` loop to create different background gradients for each of the chapter links on the left along with the arrow that will indicate the current page. This is what our single `@each` loop will produce:

The full code, along with the left-to-right gradient, is more confusing than is necessary to explain the `@each` loop functionality. Therefore, to begin with, the code we will look at will be for a solid background color. Take a look in the chapter code for the full loop with the gradient included. For now, consider the code:

```
$colors-list: $color-theme $theme-adjust-complement2 $theme-complement
$theme-adjust $theme-adjust-complement $theme-shade $theme-tint
$theme-desaturate $theme-adjust20 $theme-adjust40;

@each $current-color in $colors-list {
  $i: index($colors-list, $current-color);
  .chapter-summary {
      @include box-shadow(#ccc 1px 1px 2px);
      &:nth-child(#{$i}) {
          background-color: darken(complement(adjust-hue($current-color,
($i * 10%))), 10%);
    }
  }
}
```

Even when just using a solid background, at first glance this looks a little crazy. Let's attempt to make some sense of this.

First of all, we need a list of color values. In the chapter code, you'll see ten variables, each being a color manipulation of the pink `$theme-color` variable we created earlier in the chapter. I haven't listed the definitions of these variables above for the sake of brevity (and the actual color each variable represents isn't particularly important). We didn't have to use and reference variables there. As before, if you'd rather use color values directly (hex, RGB/HSL) that's totally fine too.

In the example, the first section of code is therefore merely a variable that is itself a list of the previous variables (remember you can see the values these variables represent in the chapter's code):

```
$colors-list: $color-theme $theme-adjust-complement2 $theme-complement
$theme-adjust $theme-adjust-complement $theme-shade $theme-tint
$theme-desaturate $theme-adjust20 $theme-adjust40;
```

With that, we can then start our `@each` loop:

```
@each $current-color in $colors-list {
    $i: index($colors-list, $current-color);
```

These two lines are actually all we need to understand. Everything after this point is generated by techniques we have already learned!

The first line effectively says, "For each color (represented by the `$current-color` variable) in the list of colors (represented by the `$colors-list` variable)". Then we open the first curly brace.

Next, is our (now familiar) friend the counter variable. The variable counter is ready to do its thing; increment with each iteration of the loop. However, unlike the `@for` loop, we're not able to explicitly state the amount of iterations we want our loop to perform. Instead, we are using a built-in SassScript function called **index**.

 There are heaps of existing SassScript functions allowing all manner of calculations, conversions, and manipulations. Check out the Sass documentation on these features at `http://sass-lang.com/docs/yardoc/Sass/Script/Functions.html`.

The `index` function counts the number of items in a list and then returns a given item's position within that list. It took me a while to wrap my head around this so in case anyone else is struggling as I did, I'll reiterate that explanation using our loop as an example.

As we have established, `$colors-list` is a variable with a number of items within it. We can therefore pass this variable to the `index` function and it will count the items within.

The part after the comma (the variable `$current-color`) will represent the item in the list and this will increment along the different list items with each iteration of the loop. That way, each iteration of the loop will select a different color from the list.

Therefore, we now have two variables at our disposal, capable of doing two things:

- The `$i` counter variable will give us a number, equivalent to the iteration number of the loop
- The `$current-color` represents the color value that has been 'selected' from the list of colors in the relevant iteration of the loop

The rest of our code is therefore just a case of placing these variables where we need them to 'print' the values we need. We won't labor over each instance a variable is used, instead let's just consider some examples

```
&:nth-child(#{$i}) {
```

Here after using the parent selector, we're incrementing the CSS `nth-child` selector to target a different element each time. Consider another example:

```
adjust-hue($current-color, ($i * 10%))
```

Here we are referencing our `$current-color` variable (remember, that's the one that changes to a different list item with each iteration of the loop) and using a little Sass math to set the value for the `adjust-hue` color transformation (the calculation is the current value of `$i` multiplied by `10%`, although we could use `10deg` and achieve the same result).

> Remember that Sass can only loop through things that exist in Sass (as used with the `index` function) or a predetermined number of items. It can't analyze the markup to determine how many items should be looped over. Therefore, when looping with Sass, ensure that you have some other means to determine the number of loops actually needed. Creating a loop of styles to produce countless possibilities (unless they are actually needed) is frankly madness. Don't let me catch you doing that!

Hopefully, having worked through those control directives, their use and syntax doesn't seem quite so baffling. Sass also has a `@while` directive for loops but we will omit covering it as I will confess I have yet to find a situation that necessitated its use. However, for the curious, take a look here: http://sass-lang.com/docs/yardoc/file.SASS_REFERENCE.html#id13

Stripping and adding units to values

When creating mixins there will be times when values need to either have their unit stripped or a unit added. Let's look at how we can do that.

Stripping the unit from a value

For example, perhaps a value returned by a function is 0%. If you want to use that as a value for a border, the % part is actually invalid CSS. Therefore we can strip the unit from a variable like this:

```
// A variable with a unit
$variable-with-unit: 0%;

// Strip the unit from the variable
$variable-without-unit: ($variable-with-unit * 0 + 1);
```

We add 0 and 1 (both without a unit) and then multiply our variable by it. This removes the unit as we are multiplying by a unit-less value.

Adding a unit to a variable value

This is how we can add a unit to a variable that represents a number:

```
// A variable with no unit
$variable-with-no-unit: 0;

// Add the unit to the variable
$variable-with-unit-added: ($variable-with-no-unit * 1%);
```

The trick is to multiply the variable by 1 unit of the type of unit you would like the value to be. In that example we have used a percentage but it could also be em or px, for example.

Writing functions in Sass

Functions are, generally speaking, most useful when creating mixins. Conceptually, the difference between the two could be described as follows; a mixin is a tool to generate a number of property and value pairs within a CSS rule. A function, on the other hand is a self contained tool to generate a value that can be used elsewhere. The result of a function can be used in a mixin or directly into the style sheet (as they can access any globally defined variables just like a mixin can).

In *Chapter 5, Responsive and Flexible Grids with Sass and Compass,* I mentioned sub-pixel rounding, a common problem with responsive grids. Before Susy had an `isolate-grid` mixin, I used a tiny grid system I'd built called 'bb-grid' to solve the sub-pixel rounding issue. It was a kind of Frankenstein of different functions, techniques, and mixins I'd taken from other grid systems to achieve my own ends.

We'll look a little at this now, simply because knowing the problems that needed to be solved will aid in explaining how a function can help.

'bb-grid' facilitates laying elements out proportionally within a row using container relative positioning. The default is left to right but the ability exists to reverse the flow of items (by changing the value of a variable) from right to left. Therefore:

- If the `$bb-flow` variable is set to `left`, the bb-grid should lay the grid items out left to right and the opposite flow would be right

- If the `$bb-flow` variable is set to `right`, the bb-grid should lay the grid items out right to left and the opposite flow would be left

Here is how a function facilitated that:

```
@function bb-opos($bb-flow) {
  @if $bb-flow == right {
    @return left;
  }
  @else {
    @return right;
  }
}
```

Now let's consider how the function works. First of all, we tell Sass we are starting a `@function` directive. Then we name the function (bb-opos in this case). Then we open parenthesis and pass the argument(s) (remember, an argument is a way to pass values to the function or mixin). In this instance, we are just using a single argument, set as the `$bb-flow` variable.

```
@function bb-opos($bb-flow) {
```

Next, within the function we are using something we are now familiar with, an `@if` and `@else` statement. Let's look at the `@if` part first:

```
@if $bb-flow == right {
    @return left;
  }
```

This part is saying, if the variable $bb-flow is equal to right (for example, $bb-flow: right;) then return the value left. That seems simple enough but there are a few things in that one statement we haven't considered before, so let's cover them now.

Equality operators

Sass supports 'equality' operators. Again, if you've had any exposure to JavaScript or PHP (in fact almost any programming language) these will be familiar:

- == means equal to (that's two equals signs)
- != means not equal to (an exclamation mark and equals sign)

The equality operators can be used on everything (strings of text and numbers).

Relational operators

Sass also allows the use of relational operators on numbers:

- < means less than
- > means greater than
- <= means less than or equal to
- => means equal to or greater than

In our preceding @if statement, we are using the equal to (==) equality operator to tell Sass that if the variable is equal to right, do the thing within the curly braces. In this instance, the thing in the curly braces is to @return left;

The @else part should now make sense:

```
@else {
    @return right;
}
```

If $bb-flow isn't set to right, then the function will return the value right.

@return

The @return directive tells Sass to return something. It's effectively the result or 'answer' if you will, of the function. As we can see above, depending upon different conditions, the value of the @return can be different. In our example, the @return can be either left or right depending upon the result of our @if and @else statement.

Ultimately however, 'there can be only one' (that's a line from 'Highlander', which despite a great soundtrack from Queen is a film franchise that started mediocre and went downhill fast) `@return` value produced by the function. It's then just a question of how we want to use it.

Using the result of a function

Now we have established what a function is, we need to consider how we can use it. With our prior example, the value returned by the function will be used to set the float value of items to either the left or the right depending upon whether the `$bb-flow` variable is set to `left` or `right`.

```
$bb-flow: left !default;
$bb-opos: bb-opos($bb-flow);
```

Here, we're setting a variable to a function. Let's consider that a little more.

There's a default value of left set for the `$bb-flow` property. On the second line is our function. It's being used to set the value of the variable `$bb-opos` to be the result (or `@return` value) of the `bb-opos` function.

Now, whenever we want to see the appropriate value that the function returns, we just reference it like this:

```
float: #{$bb-opos};
```

In that example, we're using interpolation to insert the variable `$bb-opos`. Remember that `$bb-opos` is set to be the result of our `bb-opos` function. Therefore, that property will compile to either `float: left;` or `float: right;` depending upon how the user sets the `$bb-flow` variable.

We've literally only lifted the lid on what can be done with functions in this chapter. Hopefully though, it's provided enough insight to pique your interest if the need arises.

Using the @debug directive

The `@debug` directive allows us to print values set by variables or generated by functions. However, depending on what's being used to compile Sass and Compass, you may not see them. As it's impossible to cover every possible application that can compile Sass and Compass, we'll look at how this feature works on the command line.

If not using the command line to compile Sass and Compass, it may make sense to do so momentarily. If a recap is needed, take a look at *Chapter 1*, *Getting Started with Sass and Compass*, where we noted how to browse to the relevant folder for the project you are working on and then run:

```
compass watch
```

From the command line, it's always possible to view the results of the `@debug` directive. Here's a simple example of `@debug` in action. We'll add the following at the bottom of this chapter's `_chapter-examples.scss` partial:

```
@debug $theme-complement;
```

Now, when we save the file, we can see from the command line that Compass has compiled the CSS but it also displays a message in the command line ending like this:

Chapter8/code/sass/partials/_chapter-examples.scss:46 DEBUG: #ffccd5

Here's a screenshot to illustrate this:

Sass has provided the value of that variable. Let's try another example. This time we'll debug the current value returned by the bb-opos function we looked at earlier in the chapter:

```
@debug bb-opos($bb-flow);
```

This produces a message ending like this on the command line:

Chapter8/code/sass/partials/_chapter-examples.scss:48 DEBUG: right

Here's a screenshot to illustrate this:

The @debug directive isn't something that's needed every day but it can be useful when trying to troubleshoot custom mixins and functions.

 Although we covered it in *Chapter 3, Nesting, Extend, Placeholders, and Mixins,* in case you missed it, both the Chrome Developer Tools and the FireSass plugin for Firefox provide debug info in the browser. There's a step-by-step for Chrome at http://benfra.in/1z1 and the FireSass plugin can be found at https://addons.mozilla.org/en-US/firefox/addon/firesass-for-firebug/.

The @warn directive

Sass also has a @warn directive that enjoys similar functionality to @debug. For example:

```
@warn $theme-tint;
```

Unlike @debug, messages generated by @warn can be universally suppressed by adding the following to Compass's config.rb file:

```
sass_options = {:quiet => true}
```

To re-enable warnings, either comment out the line or amend it like so:

```
sass_options = {:quiet => false}
```

Summary

In this chapter, we have had a good look at some of Sass's most complex, yet powerful capabilities. We have learned how to use control directives to create limitless loops of styles. We have also learned about interpolation and how it can be used to generate the values of variables anywhere we need them. We've also looked at functions and how we can use Sass's mathematical capabilities and operators to create logic in our style sheets.

It's fair to say we've come a long way. Despite this, the examples we have covered are fairly pedestrian. It's now up to you to take these basic concepts and bend things to your will. I know you'll do us both proud.

In our final chapter, we're going to look at some of the finer techniques we can employ with Sass and Compass and do a final code review of the styles we've written thus far. We will also consider how to switch off support for different browser vendors, use the Sass interactive shell, clear the Sass cache and a whole lot more.

Your initiation into Sass and Compass is one chapter from completion.

9
Becoming a Sass and Compass Power User

In many ways, the techniques we looked at in the last chapter are power user techniques. So why is this chapter called *Becoming a Sass and Compass Power User?* Two reasons.

Knowing so-called 'power user' techniques is one thing. However, to be truly great with a tool, requires the restraint and wisdom to know when and how to employ that tool. Therefore, before unleashing our new skills on the wide world of the Web, I think it's important we foster a 'power user' mindset to accompany them. This will include reviewing our code and considering some techniques to test and analyze our work before deploying it. That way, we will have the knowledge to understand the effects of our actions. That, my friend, is being a power user.

Secondly, this chapter won't be short of new Sass and Compass goodness. There'll be power user tricks oozing out of every fiber of this chapter. However, the new tricks and techniques we will learn in this chapter will be the kind of unrelated things that might be needed once a project, if that. Yet hopefully, knowing that they are available may be enough to dig you out of a style-sheet-shaped hole in the future.

Here are the extra 'power user' techniques we will cover:

- Turning off Compass's experimental support for differing browser vendors
- Clearing the `.sass-cache` and forcing a fresh compile
- Creating one-off compiles
- Adding the Sass globbing plugin to import batches of files
- Creating multiple separate CSS files
- Converting partials into standalone files
- Using the Sass and Compass interactive shell
- Viewing Compass style sheet and generated CSS statistics
- Avoiding performance conjecture testing
- Removing unused styles with a CSS profiler

Let's look at these 'power user' techniques first and then review our code and practices.

Turning off Compass support for specific vendors

With experimental CSS properties, it's normally necessary to use a vendor 'stack'. In a worst-case scenario, that means adding a vendor prefix version of a property for every vendor that support is necessary for.

Here is a (non-working) example with a vendor prefix for WebKit (Chrome, Safari, and now Opera too), Mozilla (Firefox), Microsoft (Internet Explorer), Opera (legacy versions), and finally the non-prefixed (official W3C) version:

```
.example {
  -webkit-property: 1px;
  -moz-property: 1px;
  -ms-property: 1px;
  -o-property: 1px;
  property: 1px;
}
```

In reality, different vendors are seldom at the same point of implementing experimental CSS features. Although it may be necessary to provide a vendor prefix for one vendor, it may not be for another.

To exemplify this, while Internet Explorer 9 had no support for CSS gradients (http://www.w3.org/TR/css3-images/#gradients), Internet Explorer 10 supports the official un-prefixed version. Therefore, although IE10 can accept the older style gradient syntax with an -ms- prefix, there seems little point including it.

Rather than take a scattergun approach and add every popular vendor prefix to every possible experimental property, the Compass team does a good job of staying on top of which experimental CSS rules require which vendor prefixes. By using Compass to author experimental CSS properties, for the most part, it's not even necessary to think about this.

However, in another scenario it may be preferable to take matters into our own hands. For example, if authoring a style sheet for a specific native mobile phone application (for example, an application that will end up the iOS, Android, or Windows phone app stores), there is little point including any vendor prefixes other than for the platform being targeted. Compass has a simple way to deal with such an eventuality.

Back in *Chapter 5*, *Responsive and Flexible Grids with Sass and Compass*, because I'm such a rebel, I opted to remove support for legacy versions of Internet Explorer in the layout grid. If you remember, it was done by adding configuration support variables in the _layout.scss partial:

```
$legacy-support-for-ie  : false;
$legacy-support-for-ie6 : $legacy-support-for-ie;
$legacy-support-for-ie7 : $legacy-support-for-ie;
```

Removing experimental support for different vendors is done in the same manner and can be done globally (meaning no properties/values get any prefixes that aren't needed).

Configuration support variables

The following is a full list of the possible configuration variables for cross-browser support and their default values. If you are happy to run with the Compass defaults, there is no need to include these variables. To re-iterate for the people sat at the back: these variables only need adding to a project if you need to change the defaults.

It's also important that if prefixes need to be removed from all Compass mixins, the support variables must be declared before Compass is imported. To exemplify, add the variables before this in the Sass files:

```
@import "compass";
```

To make changes with the following variables, simply toggle `true` and `false` depending upon your needs (notice that by default IE 6, 7, and 8 are all set to the value of the first variable, so changing that to `false` will disable all legacy IE support).

The values listed here are the Compass defaults. If nothing is changed, this is how Compass cross-vendor support is 'out of the box':

```
// Vendor support
$legacy-support-for-ie: true;
$legacy-support-for-ie6: $legacy-support-for-ie;
$legacy-support-for-ie7: $legacy-support-for-ie;
$legacy-support-for-ie8: $legacy-support-for-ie;
$experimental-support-for-mozilla: true;
$experimental-support-for-webkit: true;
$support-for-original-webkit-gradients: true;
$experimental-support-for-opera: true;
$experimental-support-for-microsoft: true;
$experimental-support-for-khtml: false;
$experimental-support-for-svg: false;
$experimental-support-for-pie: false;
$legacy-support-for-mozilla: true;
```

Most of those are fairly self-explanatory. However, of note are:

```
$support-for-original-webkit-gradients: true;
```

This is needed to support versions of the gradient syntax that were used in older Safari (prior to 5.1) and Chrome (prior to 10). If it's not necessary to support gradients on those older browser versions, disabling this can offer some code economy (as gradients are fairly verbose).

 Be aware it's likely that support for original WebKit gradients will be disabled by default in future versions of Compass.

It may also be worth disabling the following:

```
$legacy-support-for-mozilla: true;
```

This occasionally produces hacks for Firefox 3.6 and lower. The most sensible option may simply be to review your CSS output, and if you feel unneeded code is being generated, amend the variable to `false`.

Opera is now WebKit based

Finally, as Opera is now moving to WebKit (rather than using its own Presto engine) and using the `-webkit-` prefix, if support for older versions of Opera isn't needed, save a few lines of code by switching support off entirely for older Opera versions with this variable:

```
$experimental-support-for-opera: false;
```

However, be aware that Opera's Presto engine (that makes use of the `-o-` prefix) is still common on mobile devices and is likely to stay popular for many years. Therefore, if you want the widest possible support for mobile devices, leave the prefix as is.

Adding experimental support for bleeding edge CSS features

These days, CSS specifications are moving fast. It seems like every day there is an amazing new feature to try out. How can Compass keep up? Sometimes it can't but that doesn't mean it hasn't got us covered when it comes to providing support for experimental features it hasn't already got a prewritten mixin for.

Let's indulge a brief fantasy. A new property has been announced that will automatically add images of sausages behind elements. I know, I know, it'll be a massive time saver.

If such a thing did exist, here is how we might use Compass to add experimental support for different vendors:

```
.your-own-property {
  @include experimental(sausage, lincolnshire);
}
```

And here is the CSS that produces:

```
.your-own-property {
  -webkit-sausage: lincolnshire;
  -moz-sausage: lincolnshire;
  -ms-sausage: lincolnshire;
  -o-sausage: lincolnshire;
  sausage: lincolnshire;
}
```

Remember, the vendor stack produced will match what has been set with the configuration support variables.

Hopefully you can see how that worked. After including the experimental mixin, pass at least two arguments, the first being the property and the second being the value to be assigned to the property.

There are further optional arguments that can be passed to the experimental mixin and these specify the vendors that are supported. The vendor options that can be passed are: Mozilla, Webkit, Opera, Microsoft, Konquerer, and finally Official (the W3C non-prefixed version).

To illustrate, imagine we have the standard set of Compass's experimental support enabled. However, for our new faux property, sausages, Microsoft has already implemented the W3C un-prefixed version (they are all over the Sausage specification, as the use cases are so limitless).

Here's how we can write a rule that includes experimental vendor support of properties but doesn't include experimental support for Microsoft:

```
.your-own-property {
  @include experimental(sausage, lincolnshire, -moz, -webkit, -o, not
-ms, -khtml, official);
}
```

By specifying the `not` flag before the `-ms` vendor name, it removes it from the generated CSS:

```
.your-own-property {
  -webkit-sausage: lincolnshire;
  -moz-sausage: lincolnshire;
  -o-sausage: lincolnshire;
  sausage: lincolnshire;
}
```

Be aware that if the experimental support for different vendors is already set to false (by using the configuration support variables we looked at earlier), this vendor will not be output, regardless of what is passed to the mixin. To exemplify this, this is the reason that –khtml- isn't output in the preceding CSS (as support for it is disabled by default).

Here is another example. Given the following:

```
$experimental-support-for-webkit: false;

.your-own-property {
  @include experimental(sausage, lincolnshire, -moz, -webkit, not -o,
-ms, not -khtml, official);
}
```

Even though we have asked for the WebKit prefix to be added in the mixin arguments, it will not be output to the CSS. Instead, it will be omitted, along with the Opera prefix (as we have explicitly marked that to not output by using the `not` flag before the prefix) and `-khtml-` (disabled by default). Here is the actual output:

```
.your-own-property {
  -moz-sausage: lincolnshire;
  -ms-sausage: lincolnshire;
  sausage: lincolnshire;
}
```

The takeaway here, is that if the vendor stack produced does not match your expectations, double-check the configuration support variables.

Defining experimental values

Super, that has us covered for experimental properties. But what do we do if the value itself is experimental? After all, given our prior example, I'm almost certain I've not set the value of a property to `lincolnshire` before now (`float: lincolnshire;` anyone?).

Compass has a mixin to cover that. It's called `experimental-value`. Take a look at this example:

```
.your-own-property {
  @include experimental-value(sausage, lincolnshire, -moz, -webkit,
not -o, not -ms, not -khtml, official);
}
```

Here is the CSS that generates:

```
.your-own-property {
  sausage: -webkit-lincolnshire;
  sausage: -moz-lincolnshire;
  sausage: lincolnshire;
}
```

As before, it respects any global vendor support you have set alongside ones explicitly passed in as arguments.

The Sass interactive shell

By now, hopefully the **Command Line Interface** (**CLI**) doesn't seem like such a scary place. Just as well. There's a great and lesser-known Sass feature called the Sass 'interactive shell' that requires it. Let's give it a whirl.

Open the command line. Now type:

```
sass -i
```

A double-angled bracket will display like this:

```
>>
```

Excellent, we're in. Now, let's get geeky. Type this and press *Enter*:

```
mix(#fff, pink)
```

A result is 'printed' back on the command line:

```
#ffdfe5
```

How about that? The Sass interactive shell allows SassScript computations to be performed directly on the command line. Therefore, alongside any of the math we looked at in the last chapter, any of the Sass-based (but not Compass-based, more of that in a moment) color functions from *Chapter 4*, *Manipulate Color with Ease*, can be used directly in the Sass interactive shell too.

To finish working in the Sass interactive shell, just press *Ctrl + d* together to be returned to the standard command line.

I'll be honest, with the math side of things, rather than use the Sass interactive shell I find it easier to just use a calculator (or the operating system's calculator application).

However, having a quick way to perform color manipulations can be very handy.

It may initially seem frustrating that it's not possible to print the value of variables from the interactive shell. However, practically, even if there was a way to reference the current project's Sass files (perhaps by moving to that folder before starting the interactive shell) variables can change through functions so it would be impossible to know at what point the value of a variable was when we were attempting to return it.

Compass interactive

Compass has a similar command-line functionality. To perform SassScript functions within a Compass environment, run this from the command-line interface (instead of `sass -i`):

```
compass interactive
```

This will give you access to all the Compass-exclusive functions. For example, `tint` and `shade` color functions will not process using the standard Sass interactive shell but they will within the Compass-interactive environment.

Adding the Sass globbing plugin to import batches of partial files

For users who like to break their style sheets into numerous partial files, it is worth knowing that folders full of partials can be imported using a single line of code. For example, at present in the `styles.scss` file, we have the following imports listed:

```
@import "partials/variables";
@import "partials/mixins";
@import "partials/fonts";
@import "partials/normalize";
@import "partials/base";
@import "partials/placeholders";
@import "partials/bb-grid";
@import "partials/layout";
@import "partials/modules";
@import "partials/chapter-examples";
```

Instead, to import all of those partials in one go with Sass globbing, we could do this:

```
@import "partials/*";
```

However, before proceeding, know two things. Sass globbing requires installing the Sass globbing plugin (no big deal). More importantly, with globbing, files are imported in an alphabetical order. This second point is particularly important.

If the order of imports is important, using Sass globbing may not be a good idea. For example, ordinarily `normalize` or `reset` styles are at the beginning of a style sheet. With Sass globbing it's likely they will be imported near the end. Believe me when I tell you that this won't make for a happy day in the office.

In the case of the project we have been building, unless the partials are renamed to a suitable alphabetical order, an error will be reported when importing the files with globbing. This is for the exact reasons discussed. The files in our test project are order-dependent, so globbing isn't too useful here.

However, suppose we'd created a library of low-level reusable patterns that were split across multiple partial files inside a single folder and that crucially weren't order dependent. Sass globbing would make importing them all in one go a trivial exercise. Each time a new file was added to the folder there would be no need to write a further import statement.

With those caveats out of the way, let's see how it works. First, install the Sass globbing plugin. Back in the command-line interface (come on, you love it there, admit it), type this (OS X users may need to prefix with `sudo`):

```
gem install sass-globbing
```

After a moment or two something like this will be written on the command-line interface:

```
Fetching: sass-globbing-1.0.0.gem (100%)
Successfully installed sass-globbing-1.0.0
1 gem installed
```

Perfect, now in the Compass `config.rb` file (remember, this is in the root of the Sass project) add this at the top (before or after any existing `require` statements is fine):

```
require "sass-globbing"
```

Now, assuming the import files aren't order-dependent (as an example, remember that if _variables.scss needs to be loaded prior to _mixins.scss things won't go well) the prior `@import` statement will import every file within the partials folder in one go.

Creating multiple separate style sheets

The following is perhaps obvious but I feel worth explicitly stating. Suppose the need arises to supply two separate style sheets. Maybe one for small screen devices and another for large. Or perhaps one set using data URIs for image assets and another without. Whatever the reason, generating multiple, separate, CSS files can be achieved easily with Sass. Any Sass (for example, ending in `.scss`) file in the project that isn't defined as a partial (remember, the underscore before the filename indicates it is a partial) will automatically be compiled to a CSS equivalent.

Therefore, if there were three files (for example `styles.scss`, `nav-png.scss`, and `nav-svg.scss`) in the Sass folder, three CSS files will be generated (`styles.css`, `nav-png.css` and `nav-svg.css`) respectively from them.

Converting partial files to standalone style sheets

Remember that it's also easy to create a standalone file from an existing partial file. Just omit the leading underscore from the filename. So a file called `_navigation.scss` could be renamed `navigation.scss` and this would compile to `navigation.css` (if the file is still within a folder named `partials`, it will also be generated within the CSS folder in a subfolder called `partials`).

> There have been whispers in dark corridors (alright, not really, just on GitHub) that the possibility may exist in future versions of Sass to target particular styles to particular style sheets. Those curious may wish to read the following threads: `https://github.com/nex3/sass/issues/241` and `https://github.com/chriseppstein/compass/issues/664` on the Sass and Compass projects respectively.

Compass statistics

I love a good set of statistics. It turns out that Compass does too. Alongside all its other wonderful capabilities, Compass can produce statistics about a project in seconds. I like this a lot. Let me share how it's done.

> For a reminder about how to move around the command line, refer back to *Chapter 1, Getting Started with Sass and Compass*. In that chapter, we had a basic overview of how to switch folders on the command line.

First, it's necessary to move to the root of the project. The `config.rb` file lives in the root, so that's an easy flag to indicate you're at the right 'level'. When at the root of the project, run this command:

```
compass stats
```

And check out the results:

Lovely! Compass has effortlessly produced an overview of which files contain the most mixins, properties, rules, and a whole lot more. On a larger project, such information can be very instructive. However, notice that there are no statistics for the compiled CSS. Thankfully, a friendly message at the bottom (visible in this grab) indicates that we need to install css_parser to enable stats in the CSS too. Let's do that. Run the following:

```
gem install css_parser
```

After a moment, a few messages will appear ending something like the following (as ever some users may need to prefix the command with sudo):

```
Successfully installed addressable-2.3.2

Successfully installed json-1.7.7

Successfully installed rdoc-3.12.1

Successfully installed css_parser-1.2.6

4 gems installed
```

Great, at this point that's all done. Now let's run the prior command again:

```
compass stats
```

And sure enough, we now also get statistics for the generated CSS:

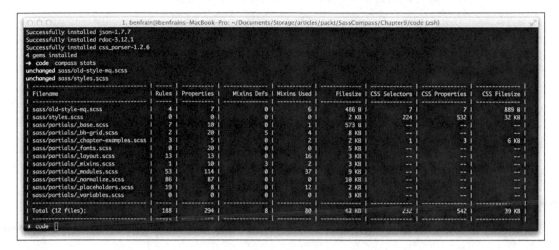

Now, when relevant data is needed to create a chart, perhaps proving to management you have been busy all day, Compass has your back.

Clearing the Sass cache

Sass uses a cache system (stored in the invisible .sass-cache folder) to speed up the creation of CSS. Very occasionally, something goes wrong in Sass and Compass land. Maybe the CSS won't generate when the Sass files are saved, or perhaps the wrong styles seem to be getting generated. If things are going pear shaped and it's not an error between the keyboard and chair, it's possible to force a clear of the Sass cache using a Compass command.

It's no exaggeration to say I've used this command less than a handful of times. However, on the off chance you need it, from the CLI, move to the root of the relevant project and run this command

```
compass clean
```

> Alternatively, you can just delete the .sass-cache folder manually (it's a hidden folder by default that lives in the root of the project) and it will be regenerated next time the Sass compiles.

One-off Compass compiles

Compass can compile to different output formats as 'one-offs'. For example, suppose while developing, it would be handy to check what the minified file size of the generated CSS is. Rather than alter the `config.rb` back and forth, we can achieve this with a command:

```
compass compile --output-style compressed --force
```

Similarly, if working with a compressed output style as standard, a one-off expanded compile could be generated as follows:

```
compass compile --output-style expanded --force
```

Mission debrief

We've covered a lot of Sass and Compass ground in our time together. At this point in building up the style sheets for `http://sassandcompass.com`, I feel the Pareto principle is coming into effect; we've covered 80% of the work with 20% of the effort. Rather than enduring the final section (sure to involve me making all manner of tedious mistakes) that wouldn't really offer any insights into using Sass and Compass, I'll be happier for you to simply grab the complete code download from the site itself.

Instead, at this point it will be more instructive to try and circumvent and address any issues we have introduced with all we have already done.

Fixing human errors

Remember that even with strong Sass and Compass-fu skills, it doesn't prevent human errors being introduced into the code. Therefore, when I feel like a project is around 70-80% styled (conveniently, the place we find ourselves), I like to take a good look at the compiled CSS and clean up all my usual schoolboy errors (there are usually plenty, so you're in good company if you are the same).

Here are some common things I look for (some we already talked about in the earlier chapters) when reviewing style sheets. These errors are not particular to Sass; they are just the usual errors that relate to writing and iterating CSS:

- Are there any normalize (or reset) styles being applied that are not required and are unlikely to ever be required? If so, comment them out. Examples in this projects code are `mark`, `table`, and `dfn`.

- Selectors should not be more than 3 levels deep (and the fewer levels the better) so reduce nesting where possible.

- Over qualified selectors should be amended so `footer[role="contentinfo"]` can just be `[role="contentinfo"]` or arguably changed to a class such as `.footer-wrap` or similar if there are styles in there that can be re-used elsewhere.

- If there are nested elements, can we help selector performance for the browser by using a child selector? So a rule such as `.chapter-summary a` (that selects all anchor links within elements that have an HTML class of `.chapter-summary`) becomes `.chapter-summary > a` (only anchors that are direct children of `.chapter-summary` are selected).

- Are any fonts being loaded that aren't required? I often try a few fonts before I settle on a 'winner', so removing the rejects makes sense from a maintainability point of view.

- Have floats and display block (or inline-block) both been added to a single element (a float declaration makes an element a block so there is no need to declare it separately)?

- Where a value of 0 is used, are there any unneeded units (for example, `0px` or `0em`)? If so, remove them.

- Have any unneeded CSS files been generated (if a partial started life as a standalone file, this often happens)?

- Have we neglected to add any pertinent pseudo classes? For example, a `:hover` pseudo class alone when we could (and perhaps should) add `:active` and `:focus` too. To remember the various link states (Link, Visited, Hover, Focus, and Active), you may find it helpful to remember the following mnemonic: *Let's Visit History For Answers* (your humble author spent an entire seven minutes thinking of that so don't let me think it was wasted).

- Has the code been commented well enough? If working on a team, this is especially important but even when flying solo, it helps to explain each section of code. That way, it has more chance of making sense when returning to it months later.

- Has the correct output style been configured? If the generated CSS is going straight to production, have we set the output style to `compressed`?

Generally speaking, these aren't necessarily problems with the way the styles will be rendered by the browser. Instead they are problems with the architecture of the code. From our perspective, we want our code to be maintainable. For the browser, we want the styles to be as effective and performant as possible, allowing the browser to paint the page quickly. Looking at the code at the end of the last chapter and comparing it to the code of this chapter should exemplify some improvements in this respect.

However, when it comes to reviewing your own project's code, consider a tool that can automate some of this process.

Catching common problems with a lint tool

JavaScript users are used to using 'lint' tools to address common problems in their code. Although, as we already know, Sass is great for catching syntax problems such as an incorrect amount of arguments being passed or an errant semicolon or curly brace, there is no way it can check for the quality of our code.

One tool to consider for this task is `http://csslint.net`. Ordinarily, **CSS Lint** is pretty unforgiving. Therefore, it's important to 'configure' CSS Lint to your preference rather than blindly follow any advice dispensed.

For example, while many things in the CSS it may take exception to are fair, some are not. For example, I'm unlikely to give up using the universal selector (*) for `box-sizing: border-box;` without a good reason!

To find out what CSS Lint thinks of your work, just copy and paste the generated CSS into the box and click **LINT!**, as shown here:

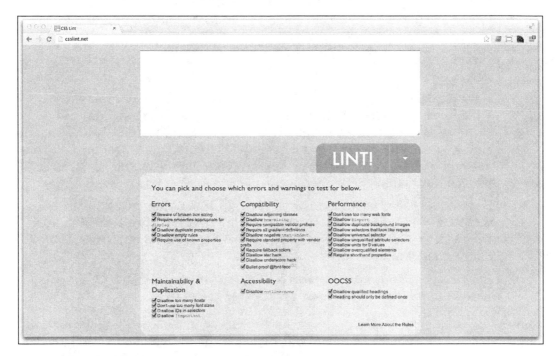

Many popular code editors (such as Sublime Text) have plugin versions of CSS Lint. Using a version in your editor of choice saves the burden of copying and pasting the generated CSS in every time. Once aware of the things you'd like it to check your CSS for, it can be a useful first-pass quality filter. Particularly when first writing in Sass.

CSScomb for property and value-pair ordering

For those anal about the ordering of property and value pairs within a rule, consider running your Sass files through **CSScomb** (`http://csscomb.com`). It enables property and value pairs to be ordered within rules in a number of predefined ways. It also comes with plugins for most major text editors.

Avoid conjecture with tools and testing

There have never been better and more accessible tools for testing CSS code before deployment. As such it's possible to supplant common performance generalizations with empirical facts. Performing tests provides actual data on which to base choices, rather than relying on mere conjecture.

To exemplify this, it has been a long-held belief that certain CSS selectors are 'slow' compared to others, the much maligned universal selector is an obvious example. Some would also argue that it would be better to use a qualified selector such as `footer[role='contentinfo']` rather than merely `[role='contentinfo']`. The theory is that in the case of the latter, the selector engine has to travel every DOM node. However such rules are typically based on generalization. For your own project, any performance difference may be of little to no consequence and the benefits of a particular selector (maintainability, low specificity) may outweigh any expected performance hit. I'll go out on a limb and suggest that in many instances, if pages appear slow, it's something entirely different causing the problem. Here's how we can find out for sure

All hail the Chrome Developer Tools

The Chrome Developer Tools have a growing number of great tools to help write more 'performant' CSS. In case you're not familiar with the Chrome Developer Tools, to find your new best friend, within Chrome, click **View | Developer | Developer Tools** from the menu (or right-click an element on screen and choose **Inspect Element** from the contextual menu).

There are similar development tools for most browsers but at present, I find the Chrome ones have more features and they are better documented.

It's important to keep in mind that the Chrome Developer Tools are only providing analysis of Chrome. Therefore while there is sure to be some performance parity with other browsers, it's not guaranteed. A feature may be expensive in one browser and not in another. As ever, testing and analysis in every browser is your friend.

Continuous page repainting

The first tool wè will look at is the 'continuous page repainting' mode. This gives an indication of how long the browser is taking to paint the page (in case there is any ambiguity, paint in this instance refers to the browser displaying what is seen on the screen), allowing the conscientious developer to eliminate costly styles.

It's worth understanding all that the Chrome Developer Tools have to offer. Take a look at the Chrome Developer Tools documentation at `https://developers.google.com/chrome-developer-tools/docs/overview`.

Furthermore, for a great introduction and primer, take a look at this free course: `http://discover-devtools.codeschool.com/`

The Chrome Developer Tools are rapidly evolving. Therefore don't be surprised if the following options are accessed in a different manner. However, the functionality of the tools is unlikely to change much and that's what we are primarily concerned with. With the Chrome Developer Tools open, click the settings 'cog' icon (bottom-right by default). Now enable the **Enable continuous page repainting** option.

This mode continually repaints the page as if there was no cache. The overlay that appears top-right provides information on how costly (in milliseconds) the page you are looking at is to render (the feint line halfway up is a control level of 16 ms — longer than that and things may need investigating). It stands to reason that more complex and larger pages (and also if displayed at a larger size) will take longer to render than smaller and simpler ones. However, all things being equal, it gives us the ability to easily toggle styles and DOM elements to see what effect they have on the page's performance. An illustration may help.

If looking at the top of the `http://sassandcompass.com` homepage we have built, the page takes around 9 ms to paint, indicated by the left-hand figure:

However, if I scroll down the page, the paint time increases dramatically to around 18 ms:

Something on the lower half of the page is therefore taking a long time to paint. And that makes me unhappy.

The easy way to find an offending item is to select it in the **Elements** panel and press the *h* key. This toggles the element on and off. In this instance, if I toggle the testimonial area, the paint time drops to 6 ms—that's some saving!

Once the offending item is found, it's then possible to investigate the style(s) that are causing the problem at a more granular level. With the rogue element selected, in the right-hand **Styles** section, simply toggle off properties until the paint time drops.

In this instance, the high paint time is being caused by a combination of `border-radius` and `drop-shadow` properties. Either one on their own reduces the paint time to around 8 ms, and that's far more acceptable. However, with both `border-radius` and `drop-shadow` on the same element, it causes the dramatic increase in paint time. Looks like I have a choice to make.

Remember, the whole point of using these tools is to test your own website and avoid relying on long standing best-practice generalizations that may not be applicable to your own situation.

To reference an earlier example, using `footer[role="contentinfo"]` is no more performant in this instance than using `[role="contentinfo"]`. Even using an ID on the element instead made only 0.1 ms difference, so the common belief that attribute selectors are slow, for Chrome at least, in this instance does not hold true.

Finding unused styles

One thing I always find I'm guilty of is introducing 'rule rot'. I'm not sure what the correct terminology for this is. It's how I describe the situation whereby surplus HTML classes in the markup, or rules in the style sheets have been added. It's typically a byproduct of refactoring code. Thankfully, there are now tools that can help with some housekeeping in this respect.

My favorite is the CSS profiles feature in Chrome Developer Tools. Let's use it to see where I have generated unneeded rules.

Within Chrome, open the Developer Tools. Along the top of the Developer Tools window, click the **Profiles** tab. A window, something like this, will appear:

Ensure that **Collect CSS Selector Profile** is selected and click **Start**. Now use browse the site/page in question thoroughly. Hover over links, visit all the different pages of the site and resize the browser window so that any media query-based rules are triggered. When confident everything has been triggered, click the big red stop button (bottom left).

On the left side, there is now a profile recorded. Click this and a list of selectors will be displayed.

You can now sort the various columns. **Matches** is the column of interest for now. Click it twice and selectors with no matches will be at the top.

The key now is to find any rules that have a source file listed (for example styles. css) and have zero matches. These are the rules in the style sheet that have not been used and can potentially be removed from the style sheets.

There's still work to be done investigating whether or not these rules can be removed, but it provides a handy quick start (by the way, you can also select all the contents of a profile and paste it into a spreadsheet if you like).

Parting shots

Now that we have looked at how to quality check our style sheets and performed some testing to make it more performant, let's bring things back to Sass and Compass. Grasshopper, before we say 'sayonara', I'd like to remind you that getting the most out of Sass and Compass isn't about employing every single feature at every single opportunity. After all, it's supposed to make authoring style sheets easier and more enjoyable.

Therefore, when using it for the first time on a live project, only use the things that actually help you. Don't worry if writing a mixin to produce a certain set of styles doesn't work straight off the bat. Enjoy the things that help right away. Perhaps it's as simple as defining all the project's colors as variables, or simply producing cross-vendor CSS effortlessly with some existing Compass mixins. Grow your confidence in wielding Sass and Compass to make life easier first and foremost and then throw in the extra ingredients (loops, globbing, sprites, data URIs, and more) as you feel braver.

Summary

I'd like to share a quote from Michael Crichton's book *Jurassic Park*:

> *Your scientists were so preoccupied with whether or not they could, they didn't stop to think if they should.*

This is instructive, not just of the incredibly highbrow prose I read, but perhaps also the situation you now find yourself in. If your humble author has done even a half decent job, you should have gained an understanding of most of the major functionality and techniques available when using Sass and Compass to author style sheets.

Just be mindful that although we have these skills and techniques at our disposal, this doesn't necessarily mean they are right to use all the time.

Practically, we have already considered that things such as over-nesting rules can produce anti-patterns in our generated code. In the same vein, consider whether other practices that are now more easily achievable with Sass and Compass are actually the right choice. In-lining a 1 MB image as a data URI in your CSS wouldn't be a smart move, for example. I know you'll make the right choices.

With that fatherly advice squared away, my primary wish is that you now feel empowered and not intimidated by all that Sass and Compass has to offer. Remember, it exists to make things easier and not more difficult. Now that your Sass and Compass powers are strong, it's time for you to go forth and create amazing things.

Until next time.

Index

Symbols

A

B

C

nested output option 41, 42
nest rules, Sass 12, 13
non-SVG capable devices 192
nth-omega mixin 138, 139

O

oily_png 182
Opera
    about 225
    WebKit based 225

P

package
    installing, for Mac OS X 18
padding
    around images 185
pad mixin 135, 136
partial file
    about 45
    converting, to standalone style sheets 231
    creating 45, 46
    creating, for fonts 67, 68
    importing 48
    using 45, 46
paths
    setting, for project assets 40
placeholder selectors
    used, for extending styles 77, 78
plugin.js file 168
post mixin 136
prefix mixin 133
pre mixin 136
project
    Susy, including in 120
project assets
    name. setting for 40
    paths, setting for 40
project variables, Susy 120, 121
pull mixin 137
push mixin 137

R

Red Green Blue Alpha. *See* RGBA
relational operators 215

relative assets
    enabling 44
responsive grid
    creating, for mobile 125
result
    using, of functions 216
RGBA 11
Ruby
    installing, on Windows 19
rules
    extending, @extend directive used 75-77

S

Salsa grid system 117
Sass
    about 7, 15
    colors, defining as variables 10
    comment formats 50
    functions, writing 213, 215
    graphical tools 26
    installing 17
    latest version, installing 23, 24
    maintainability feature 46, 47
    math calculations 200-202
    nest rules 12, 13
    production ready code 46, 47
    syntax, for writing variables 49, 50
    URL 15
    using 9
    variables, syntax 10
    versions 22
Sass and Compass framework
        Foundation 3 117
Sass-based project
    creating, from command line 24, 25
    setting up 34
Sass cache
    clearing 233
Sass files
    working, in text editors 30
Scout 26, 27
selectors 168
single line comments 50, 51
span-columns mixin 133
SPDY 46

Thank you for buying
Sass and Compass for Designers

About Packt Publishing

Packt, pronounced 'packed', published its first book "*Mastering phpMyAdmin for Effective MySQL Management*" in April 2004 and subsequently continued to specialize in publishing highly focused books on specific technologies and solutions.

Our books and publications share the experiences of your fellow IT professionals in adapting and customizing today's systems, applications, and frameworks. Our solution based books give you the knowledge and power to customize the software and technologies you're using to get the job done. Packt books are more specific and less general than the IT books you have seen in the past. Our unique business model allows us to bring you more focused information, giving you more of what you need to know, and less of what you don't.

Packt is a modern, yet unique publishing company, which focuses on producing quality, cutting-edge books for communities of developers, administrators, and newbies alike. For more information, please visit our website: www.packtpub.com.

Writing for Packt

We welcome all inquiries from people who are interested in authoring. Book proposals should be sent to author@packtpub.com. If your book idea is still at an early stage and you would like to discuss it first before writing a formal book proposal, contact us; one of our commissioning editors will get in touch with you.

We're not just looking for published authors; if you have strong technical skills but no writing experience, our experienced editors can help you develop a writing career, or simply get some additional reward for your expertise.

Responsive Web Design with HTML5 and CSS3

ISBN: 978-1-849693-18-9   Paperback: 324 pages

Learn responsive design using HTML5 and CSS3 to adapt websites to any browser or screen size

1.   Everything needed to code websites in HTML5 and CSS3 that are responsive to every device or screen size

2.   Learn the main new features of HTML5 and use CSS3's stunning new capabilities including animations, transitions and transformations

3.   Real world examples show how to progressively enhance a responsive design while providing fall backs for older browsers

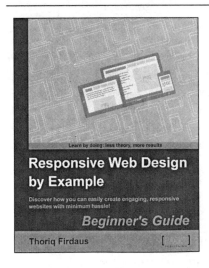

Responsive Web Design by Example

ISBN: 978-1-849695-42-8   Paperback: 338 pages

Discover how you can easily create engaging, responsive websites with minimum hassle!

1.   Rapidly develop and prototype responsive websites by utilizing powerful open source frameworks

2.   Focus less on the theory and more on results, with clear step-by-step instructions, previews, and examples to help you along the way

3.   Learn how you can utilize three of the most powerful responsive frameworks available today: Bootstrap, Skeleton, and Zurb Foundation

Please check **www.PacktPub.com** for information on our titles

jQuery Hotshot

ISBN: 978-1-849519-10-6   Paperback: 296 pages

Ten practical projects that exercise your skill, build your confidence, and help you master jQuery

1. See how many of jQuery's methods and properties are used in real situations. Covers jQuery 1.9.

2. Learn to build jQuery from source files, write jQuery plugins, and use jQuery UI and jQuery Mobile.

3. Familiarize yourself with the latest related technologies like HTML5, CSS3, and frameworks like Knockout.js.

Instant SASS CSS How-to

ISBN: 978-1-782163-78-7   Paperback: 80 pages

Learn to write more efficient CSS with the help of the SASS CSS library using practical, hands-on recipes

1. Learn something new in an Instant! A short, fast, focused guide delivering immediate results.

2. Learn how to download and install SASS and compile SASS code to validate CSS

3. Learn how to use the various elements of SASS, such as mixins, variables, control directives, and functions to create valid CSS

4. Use an external mixin library such as Compass with SASS to produce exciting effects and learn to create your own mixin library

Please check **www.PacktPub.com** for information on our titles

CPSIA information can be obtained at www.ICGtesting.com
Printed in the USA
BVOW06s1546270713

327120BV00003B/103/P